# Bugs, Bugs, Bugs!

Pam Schiller

Special Needs Adaptations by Clarissa Willis

# Acknowledgments

I would like to thank the following people for their contributions to this book. The special needs adaptations were written by Clarissa Willis. The CD is arranged by Patrick Brennan, and performed by Richele Bartkowiak and Patrick Brennan. It was engineered and mixed by Jeff Smith at Southwest Recordings. —Pam Schiller

Clarissa Willis

Patrick Brennan

Richele Bartkowiak

# Books written by Pam Schiller

*The Bilingual Book of Rhymes, Songs, Stories, and Fingerplays,* with Rafael Lara-Alecio and Beverly J. Irby

*The Complete Book of Activities, Games, Stories, Props, Recipes, and Dances,* with Jackie Silberg

*The Complete Book of Rhymes, Songs, Poems, Fingerplays, and Chants,* with Jackie Silberg

*The Complete Daily Curriculum for Early Childhood: Over 1200 Easy Activities to Support Multiple Intelligences and Learning Styles,* with Pat Phipps

*The Complete Resource Book: An Early Childhood Curriculum,* with Kay Hastings

*The Complete Resource Book for Infants: Over 700 Experiences for Children From Birth to 18 Months*

*The Complete Resource Book for Toddlers and Twos: Over 2000 Experiences and Ideas*

*Count on Math: Activities for Small Hands and Lively Minds,* with Lynne Peterson

*Creating Readers: Over 1000 Games, Activities, Tongue Twisters, Fingerplays, Songs, and Stories to Get Children Excited About Reading*

*Do You Know the Muffin Man?,* with Thomas Moore

*The Instant Curriculum, Revised,* with Joan Rosanno

*The Practical Guide to Quality Child Care,* with Patricia Carter Dyke

*Start Smart: Building Brain Power in the Early Years*

*The Values Book,* with Tamera Bryant

*Where Is Thumbkin?,* with Thomas Moore

CD INSIDE!

# Bugs, Bugs, Bugs!

## 21 Songs and Over 250 Activities for Young Children

by Pam Schiller

**Gryphon House, Inc.**
**Beltsville, Maryland**

## Bulk purchase

Gryphon House books are available for special premiums and sales promotions as well as for fundraising use. Special editions or book excerpts also can be created to specification. For details, contact the Marketing Director at Gryphon House.

# Bugs, Bugs, Bugs!

© 2006 Pam Schiller
Printed in the United States of America.

Illustrations: Deborah Johnson
Cover Art: © 2002 Getty Images, Inc. gettyimages.com

Published by Gryphon House, Inc.
10726 Tucker Street, Beltsville, MD 20705
301.595.9500; 301.595.0051 (fax); 800.638.0928 (toll-free)

Visit us on the web at www.gryphonhouse.com

 Gryphon House is a member of the Green Press Initiative, a nonprofit program dedicated to supporting publishers in their efforts to reduce their use of fiber sourced forests. For further information visit www.greenpressinitiative.org

## Library of Congress Cataloging-in-Publication Data

Schiller, Pamela Byrne.
  Bugs, bugs, bugs! / Pam Schiller and Richele Bartkowiak ; illustrations, Deborah Johnson.
      p. cm.
  Includes bibliographical references and index.
  ISBN-13: 978-0-87659-020-1
  ISBN-10: 0-87659-020-2
  1.  Language arts (Early childhood)--Activity programs. 2.  Children's songs. 3.  Early childhood education--Activity programs.  I. Johnson, Deborah, ill. II. Title.
    LB1139.5.L35S35 2006
    372.21--dc22

                                    2006003272

# Table of Contents

# Introduction

## Music in the Early Years

Music is a universal language, and singing is a hallmark of the early childhood classroom. Children love to sing! Teachers love to sing! Age makes no difference. Culture makes no difference.

Singing songs enriches thematic content, supports literacy concepts, and optimizes memory and learning. When you extend classroom activities, including modifications for special needs and English language learner populations, it is a perfect package. *Bugs, Bugs, Bugs!* is one of eight thematic book/CD sets that offer all of these resources in one package.

## Thematic Content

*Bugs, Bugs, Bugs!* overlaps several typical early childhood themes, including Insects, Bugs, and Health and Safety. Read the lyrics and decide the best fit in your curriculum for each song.

Each song is accompanied by a list of facts titled "Did You Know?" which offers background information about the song, interesting facts about the topic or lyrics, historical information, or some form of trivia you might use as a springboard to discussion. This will save you hours of research and add significantly to the value of the song.

## Literacy Concepts

Young children need experiences that allow them to develop and practice basic literacy skills, such as listening, oral language development, phonological awareness, letter knowledge, print awareness, and comprehension. Suggestions for using the songs in *Bugs, Bugs, Bugs!* as a springboard for teaching these literacy skills accompany every title. Below is a definition of each literacy skill and the sub-skills they encompass.

○ **Listening:** the development of age-appropriate attention span, as well as the ability to listen for a variety of purposes; for example, details, directions, and sounds.

○ **Oral Language Development:** the acquisition of vocabulary, the fine-tuning of grammar, and the increase in sentence length and complexity.

○ **Phonological Awareness:** sensitivity to the sounds of language. Phonological awareness begins with babbling and cooing and goes all the way through the understanding of sound and symbol relationships and decoding. The skills in the higher end of the phonological awareness continuum—sound and symbol relationship and decoding—are appropriate for children who are age five or older.

○ **Segmentation:** the breaking apart of words by syllable or letter; for example, children clap the breaks in the word *di-no-saur.*

○ **Rhyme:** words that sound alike. The ending sound of the words is the same, but the initial consonant sound is different, for example, *cat* and *hat,* or *rake* and *cake.*

○ **Alliteration:** the repetition of a consonant sound in a series of words; for example, *Peter Piper picked a peck of pickled peppers.* Children need to be able to hear the repetition of the /p/ sound, but do not need to identify that the sound is made by the letter "p".

○ **Onomatopoeia:** words that sound suggest the sound they are describing; for example, *pitter-patter, moo, quack, beep,* and so on.

○ **Letter Knowledge:** the visual recognition of each letter of the alphabet, both lowercase and uppercase.

○ **Print Awareness:** the understanding that print has many functions; for example, telling a story, making a list, as part of signs, in news articles, in recipes, and so on. It is also the awareness that print moves left to right and top to bottom.

○ **Comprehension:** the internalization of a story or a concept.

# Optimizing Memory and Learning

Singing boosts memory and keeps the brain alert. Increased memory and alertness optimize the potential for learning. When we sing we generally feel good. That sense of well-being causes the brain to release endorphins into the blood stream and those endorphins act as a memory fixative. When we sing we automatically increase our oxygen intake, which, in turn, increases our alertness. Scientific research has validated what early childhood professionals know intuitively—that singing has a positive effect on learning.

# Expanding Children's Learning With Activities

Using songs as a springboard for activities is a good way to bring the lyrics of the song into a meaningful context for children. Exploring different types of clothing after singing a song about winter clothes reinforces and creates a meaningful context for the specific characteristics of winter clothing. Observing ants in a jar after singing "Little Ants" reinforces and creates meaningful context for the specific characteristics of this type of insect. Making "playdough worms," creating a wormy snack, moving items across the floor like a worm, observing live worms, and measuring classroom materials with pretend worms after singing "Nobody Likes Me" helps children better understand the characteristics of worms, as well as the role worms play in the environment.

Reading a book about worms after singing about worms also helps expand children's understanding. Literature selections are provided for each song. Integrating the teaching of themes and skills with songs, literature, and multidisciplinary activities provides a comprehensive approach for helping children recognize the patterns and the interconnected relationships of what they are learning.

Throughout the book, questions to ask children appear in italics. These questions are intended to help children think and reflect on what they have learned. This reflective process optimizes the opportunity for children to apply the information and experiences they have encountered.

# Modifications

Suggestions for children with special needs and suggestions for English language learners accompany the song activities when appropriate. These features allow teachers to use the activities with diverse populations. All children love to sing and the benefits apply to all!

## Special Needs

The inclusion of children with disabilities in preschool and child care programs is increasingly common. Parents, teachers, and researchers have found that children benefit in many ways from integrated programs that are designed to meet the needs of all children. Many children with disabilities, however, need accommodations to participate successfully in the general classroom.

Included in the extensions and activities for each song are adaptations for children with special needs. These adaptations allow *all* children to experience the song and related activities in a way that will maximize their learning opportunities. The adaptations are specifically for children who have needs in the following areas:

- O sensory integration
- O distractibility
- O hearing loss
- O spatial organization
- O language, receptive and expressive
- O fine motor coordination
- O cognitive challenges

The following general strategies from Kathleen Bulloch (2003) are for children who have difficulty listening and speaking.

| Difficulty | Adaptations/Modifications/Strategies |
|---|---|
| Listening | o State the objective—provide a reason for listening<br>o Use a photo card<br>o Give explanations in small, discrete steps<br>o Be concise with verbal information: "Evan, please sit," instead of "Evan, would you please sit down in your chair?"<br>o Provide visuals<br>o Have the child repeat directions<br>o Have the child close his eyes and try to visualize the information<br>o Provide manipulative tasks<br>o When giving directions to the class, leave a pause between each step so the child can carry out the process in her mind<br>o Shorten the listening time required<br>o Pre-teach difficult vocabulary and concepts |
| Verbal Expression | o Provide a prompt, such as beginning the sentence for the child or giving a picture cue<br>o Accept an alternate form of information-sharing, such as artistic creation, photos, charade or pantomime, and demonstration<br>o Ask questions that require short answers<br>o Specifically teaching body and language expression<br>o First ask questions at the information level—giving facts and asking for facts back<br>o Wait for children to respond; don't call on the first child to raise his hand<br>o Have the child break in gradually by speaking in smaller groups and then in larger groups |

### English Language Learners

Strategies for English language learners are also provided to maximize the learning potential for English language learners.

The following are general strategies for working with English language learners (Gray, Fleischman, 2004-05):

○ **Keep the language simple.** Speak simply and clearly. Use short, complete sentences in a normal tone of voice. Avoid using slang, idioms, or figures of speech.

○ **Use actions and illustrations to reinforce oral statements.** Appropriate prompts and facial expressions help convey meaning.

○ **Ask for completion, not generation.** Ask children to choose answers from a list or to complete a partially finished sentence. Encourage children to use language as much as possible to gain confidence over time.

○ **Model correct usage and judiciously correct errors.** Use corrections to positively reinforce children's use of English. When English language learners make a mistake or use awkward language, they are often attempting to apply what they know about their first language to English. For example, a Spanish-speaking child may say, "It fell from me," a direct translation from Spanish, instead of "I dropped it."

○ **Use visual aids.** Present classroom content and information in a way that engages children—by using graphic organizers (word web, story maps, KWL charts), photographs, concrete materials, and graphs, for example.

# Involving English Language Learners in Music Activities

Music is a universal language that draws people together. For English language learners, music can be a powerful vehicle for language learning and community-building. Music and singing are important to second language learners for many reasons, including:

○ The rhythms of music help children hear the sounds and intonation patterns of a new language.

○ Musical lyrics and accompanying motions help children learn new vocabulary.

○ Repetitive patterns of language in songs help children internalize the sentence structure of English.

○ Important cultural information is conveyed to young children in the themes of songs.

Strategies for involving English language learners in music activities vary according to the children's level of proficiency in the English language.

| Level of Proficiency | Strategies |
| --- | --- |
| Beginning English Language Learners | ○ Keep the child near you and model motions as you engage in group singing.<br>○ Use hand gestures, movements, and signs as often as possible to accompany song lyrics, making sure to tie a specific motion to a specific word.<br>○ Refer to real objects in the environment that are named in a song.<br>○ Stress the intonation, sounds, and patterns in language by speaking the lyrics of the song while performing actions or referring to objects in the environment.<br>○ Use simple, more common vocabulary. For example, use round instead of circular. |
| Intermediate-Level English Language Learners | ○ Say the song before singing it, so children can shear the words and rhythms of the lyrics.<br>○ Use motions, gestures, and signs to help children internalize the meaning of song lyrics. Be sure the motion is tied clearly to the associated word.<br>○ Throughout the day, repeat the language patterns found in songs in various activities.<br>○ Stress the language patterns in songs, and pause as children fill in the blanks.<br>○ Adapt the patterns of song, using familiar vocabulary. |
| Advanced English Language Learners | ○ Use visuals to cue parts of a song.<br>○ Use graphic organizers to introduce unfamiliar information.<br>○ Use synonyms for words heard in songs to expand children's vocabulary.<br>○ Develop vocabulary through description and comparison. For example, it is round like a circle. It is circular.<br>○ Encourage children to make up new lyrics for songs. |

# How to Use This Book

Use the twenty-six songs on the *Bugs, Bugs, Bugs!* and the related activities in this book to enhance themes in your curriculum, or use them independently. Either way you have a rich treasure chest of creative ideas for your classroom.

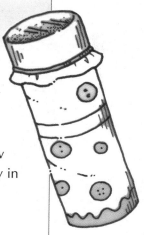

The eight-package collection provides more than 200 songs, a perfect combination of the traditional best-loved children's songs and brand new selections created for each theme. Keep a song in your heart and put joy in your teaching!

# Bibliography

Bulloch, K. 2003. *The mystery of modifying: Creative solutions.* Huntsville, TX: Education Service Center, Region VI.

Cavallaro, C. & M. Haney. 1999. *Preschool inclusion.* Baltimore, MD: Paul H. Brookes Publishing Company.

Gray, T. and S. Fleischman. Dec. 2004-Jan. 2005. "Research matters: Successful strategies for English language learners." *Educational Leadership,* 62, 84-85.

Hanniford, C. 1995. *Smart moves: Why learning is not all in your head.* Arlington, VA: Great Ocean Publications, p. 146.

LeDoux, J. 1993. "Emotional memory systems in the brain." *Behavioral and Brain Research,* 58.

Tabors, P. 1997. *One child, two languages: Children learning English as a second language.* Baltimore, MD: Paul H. Brookes Publishing Company.

# Songs and Activities

# Baby Bumblebee

I caught myself a baby bumblebee.
Won't my mommy be so proud of me!
I caught myself a baby bumblebee.
Ouch! He stung me!
I'm talking to my baby bumblebee.
Won't my mommy be so proud of me!
I'm talking to my baby bumblebee.
"Oh," he said, "I'm sorry."
I let go of my baby bumblebee.
Won't my mommy be so proud of me!
I let go of my baby bumblebee.
Look, he's happy to be free!

**Special Needs Adaptation:** This song provides an excellent opportunity for children with special needs to learn kindness to animals while working on generalization skills. These skills enable the child to apply information learned in one experience or setting to information or activities in another setting. Show the child a picture of a bumblebee and talk about how the child in the song was kind to the bee by letting it go. Next, show the child pictures of animals he may come in contact with in his daily life, such as a dog, cat, or bird. If there is a class pet, such as a hamster, gerbil, or fish, talk about what the child can do to be kind to the animal. Model how to hold or feed the animal. Explain that it is unkind to feed an animal too much food or the wrong kind of food. Talk about the importance of using a soft touch with animals. Explain that it is cruel to hit or grab them.

## Vocabulary

baby
bumblebee
free
happy
mommy
ouch
proud
sorry
stung

## Theme Connections

Feelings
Friends and Families

## Did You Know?

○ A bumblebee is a small creature, ¾ to 1 ½ inches (19-38mm) long.
○ Bumblebees are usually black and yellow.
○ Bumblebees collect and carry pollen to the hive on their hind legs.
○ Bumblebee colonies are a spectacular example of social organization, with each member working tirelessly to protect and build the colony.
○ Bumblebees are normally docile and non-aggressive while pollinating flowers, but turn vicious when their nests are disturbed. They will chase intruders away from their nest for several yards.
○ See page 51 in "The Bee and the Pup" for additional information about bumblebees.

# Literacy Links

### Letter Knowledge

○ Print *bumblebee* on chart paper. Encourage the children to identify and count how many times the letter "b" occurs in the word.

### Oral Language

○ Sing the original version of the song (page 92). Discuss the differences in the versions. Which version do the children like better?

○ Discuss kindness to animals. Invite children to talk about interesting bugs they have found. Remind the children that bumblebees should never be disturbed.

○ Teach the children the American Sign Language sign for *bee* (page 121).

### Phonological Awareness

○ Write *baby bumblebee* on chart paper. Underline the first letter in each word. Have the children say the words. Can they hear the repetition of the /b/ sound? Point out that the repetition of a beginning sound in a series of words is called *alliteration*. Have the children say, "Baby bumblebees buzz like bullets." Do they hear the repetition of the /b/ sound?

### Segmentation

○ Say "bumblebee." Clap the syllables in the word. Ask the children to name other bugs and clap the syllables in the names.

# Curriculum Connections

### Discovery

○ Show the children a honeycomb. Invite them to take a close-up look with a magnifying glass.

### Language

○ Copy the Bee Pattern (page 105) from the Bug Pattern Cards (pages 105-106) so each child can make a puppet. Have the children color and cut out their bees. Help them glue the bee to a tongue depressor. Challenge the children to follow your directions with their puppets. For example, hold your bee *over* your head, *behind* your back, *beside* a friend, *on top of* your hand, *below* your knee, and so on.

## Book Corner

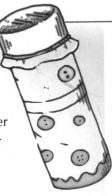

### Listening

○ Invite the children to make kazoos. Give each child an empty toilet paper tube, a rubber band, and a circle of wax paper. Help them wrap the wax paper circle around one end of the toilet paper tube and secure it with a rubber band. Show them how to make a buzzing sound with their kazoos and then encourage them to "buzz, buzz, buzz!"

### Music and Movement

○ Teach the children how to do the Waggle Dance. This dance is inspired by bees as they gather pollen from flowers. The children ("bees") wiggle their bottoms like bees to communicate to other "bees" where pollen is located. They wiggle as they circle around a paper flower (pollen) in the center of the floor. Play classical music. Have the children spread their wings (arms) and wiggle their bottoms as they fly around the flower. Change the location of the flower and start the dance again.

### Science

○ Provide a picture of a bee. Photocopy and laminate the Rebus Insect Checklist (page 118). Encourage the children to check the list to see if the bee is a true insect with three body parts, two antennae, six legs, and an outer skeleton.

### Snack

○ Invite the children to use the Honey Balls Rebus (page 98) to make their snack.

### Story Time

○ Use the Puppet Patterns (page 101) to tell children the story of "Bessie Bee's Bell" (page 94).

### Writing

○ Print *bumblebee* on several sheets of paper, leaving a blank place where the letter b's belong. Provide magnetic letters and encourage the children to fill in the blanks.

# Home Connection

○ Encourage children to look for bees outside their homes. Remind them to keep a safe distance from the bees and not to disturb them in any way.

# Mosquitoes

## Vocabulary

arm
bite
camp
damp
face
mosquitoes
swarms
taste
wet
wing

## Theme Connections

Camping
Movement
Parts of the Body

(Tune: Mary Had a Little Lamb)
Mosquitoes like it wet and damp,
Wet and damp, wet and damp.
Mosquitoes like it wet and damp.
They hang out where you camp.
Mosquitoes fly around in swarms,
Around in swarms, around in swarms.
Mosquitoes fly around in swarms.
They have wings for arms.
Mosquitoes bite your arms and face,
Arms and face, arms and face.
Mosquitoes bite your arms and face.
They like the way you taste.

## Did You Know?

❍ Male mosquitoes do not bite. The female bites in order to extract a meal of blood to help in the production of her eggs.

❍ Depending on the species, a female mosquito may lay between 100 and 300 eggs in her lifetime.

❍ Mosquitoes lay their eggs in wet, damp places, such as lakes, streams, ditches, ponds, salt land marshes, empty containers, and old tires.

❍ See page 28 in "My Pet Mosquito" for additional information on mosquitoes.

## Literacy Links

### Oral Language

❍ Discuss *wet* and *damp*. *How is damp the same as wet? Is it different?* Demonstrate the difference between wet and damp.

❍ Teach the children the American Sign Language sign for *mosquito* (page 122).

### Phonological Awareness

❍ Encourage children to find the rhyming word pairs in the song— *damp/camp* and *face/taste*.

# Curriculum Connections

### Discovery

- ❍ Dampen a towel. Challenge the children to think of ways to dry the towel; for example, place it in the sun, place it under a light, or swing it through the air.

- ❍ Use the Mosquito Life Span Sequence Cards (pages 112-114) to discuss the life cycle of the mosquito. First, the female mosquito drops her eggs into water. A wriggler hatches from each egg. It eats tiny animals in the water. In a week, the wriggler changes into a pupa which floats just under the water. In a few days the pupa's skin splits down the back. A winged adult mosquito comes out. Challenge the children to sequence the cards.

### Dramatic Play

- ❍ Set up a camping site. Encourage the children to pretend that they are camping. Label a clean spray container "mosquito repellent" and place it with the camping supplies. Suggest plots for their play.

### Games

- ❍ Make two photocopies of the Bug Pattern Cards (pages 105-106). Color them, cut them out, and laminate them. Give the cards to the children and encourage them to play Bug Concentration.

  ✓ **Special Needs Adaptation:** Enlarge the bug cards to make them easy to use by children who have physical limitations. For children with cognitive challenges, use fewer cards. For children who are unable to understand the concept of the game, make two copies of the Bug Pattern Cards. Color one set of Bug Pattern Cards one color and the other set another color. Invite the child to see if he can match the bugs to the identical card of another color.

## Book Corner

*Mosquito* by Jennifer
   Coldrey
*Mosquitoes* by Julie
   Murray
*Why Mosquitoes
   Buzz in People's
   Ears* by Verna
   Aardema

### Outdoor Play

○ Teach the children to play Fly By; Go Mosquito. Make a start and finish line approximately 25' apart. Have the children stand on the start line. Assign half of the group to be mosquitoes and the other half to be children. Instruct the children to begin to fly when you say, "Fly by." After a few seconds, say, "Go mosquitoes" to signal the mosquitoes that it is time to try to catch one of the children. If the children make it to the finish line without being tagged they are safe. If a mosquito catches a child before he or she makes it to the finish line, the child becomes a mosquito. Continue until all of the children become mosquitoes or until the children tire of the game.

### Science

○ Show the children a picture of a mosquito. Challenge them to use the Rebus Insect Checklist (page 118) to determine if the mosquito is an insect. *Does the mosquito have three body parts, two antennae, six legs, and an outer skeleton?*

### Snack

○ Invite the children to use the Mosquito Shake Rebus (page 99) to prepare snack.

 **English Language Learner Strategy:** Using a rebus makes it easier for English language learners to follow the directions.

### Water Play

○ Provide items that can be used to suck up water, such as eyedroppers, basters, and syringes. Encourage the children to pretend they are mosquitoes enjoying a meal!

### Writing

○ Print *mosquito* on drawing paper. Provide an eyedropper and red water (use red food coloring or red tempera paint in water) to represent blood. Encourage the children to trace over *mosquito* by releasing drops of "blood" over the letters.

# Home Connection

○ Make photocopies of the Mosquito Life Span Sequence Cards (pages 112-114) for each child. Send a set home so the children can use the cards to tell their families what they know about mosquitoes.

# The Ants Go Marching

The ants go marching one by one,
Hurrah, hurrah.
The ants go marching one by one,
Hurrah, hurrah.
The ants go marching one by one.
The little one stops to suck his thumb.
And they all go marching down,
To the ground,
To get out of the rain.
BOOM! BOOM! BOOM!

Additional verses:
…two…tie her shoe…
…three…climb a tree…
…four…shut the door…
…five…take a dive…

BOOM! BOOM!

## Vocabulary

| | |
|---|---|
| ants | one |
| boom | rain |
| dive | shoe |
| door | suck |
| five | three |
| four | thumb |
| ground | tree |
| march | two |

## Theme Connections

Counting
Movement
Sounds

## Did You Know?

○ Like all insects, ants have six legs. Each leg has three joints. Ants have strong legs, which enable them to run very quickly. If people could run as fast as an ant relative to their size, they could run as fast as a racehorse.
○ Ants have two eyes; each eye is made of many smaller eyes called compound eyes.
○ An ant's head has a pair of large, strong jaws. Their jaws open and shut sideways like a pair of scissors. Adult ants cannot chew or swallow solid food. Instead, they swallow juices that they squeeze from pieces of food. They throw away the dry leftover part.
○ Ants use their antennae for touch and for their sense of smell.
○ See page 59 in "Little Ants" and page 39 in "Little Ant's Hill" for additional information about ants.

## Literacy Links

### Oral Language
○ Discuss ants. *What do they eat? Where do they live? How do they move?*
○ Teach the children the American Sign Language sign for *ant* (page 121).

### Phonological Awareness

O Sing the song, stopping occasionally to let the children fill in the rhyming word that matches the numeral.

✓ **English Language Learner Strategy:** Partner the English language learner with a child who is proficient in English and together they can find rhyming words that match the numeral.

### Print Awareness

O Ask the children to brainstorm a list of all of the activities an ant can do; for example, walk, carry, lift, climb, build, dig, eat, and sleep. Print the children's ideas on chart paper.

# Curriculum Connections

### Discovery

O Show the children how to make fingerprint ants. Place an ink pad or fingerpaint on the table. Have the children press their finger in the ink or the fingerpaint and then onto drawing paper three times to make an ant body. Provide markers so the children can add legs and antennae.

### Fine Motor

O Invite a group of older children to teach the children to tie their shoes.

O Photocopy the ant from the Bug Pattern Cards (page 106). Color it, cut it out, laminate it, and glue a large paper clip to its back. Prepare a 10" x 12" sheet of cardboard. Draw underground ant tunnels on it. Place the ant on top of the cardboard. Provide a large magnet and show the children how to move the ant through the maze by moving the magnet under the cardboard.

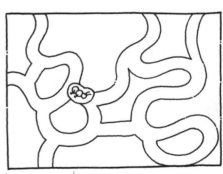

### Gross Motor

O Add a few drops of vanilla extract to a few cotton balls. Place these scented cotton balls on the floor in a trail. Place a few unscented cotton balls on another trail. Remind the children that ants follow a trail by using their sense of smell. When an ant finds food, it runs back to the anthill to "tell" the other ants. As it runs, it leaves a trail the other ants in the hill can smell. The ants find the food by smelling their way along the trail. Have the children follow the trail of cotton balls by using their sense of smell. To make this more challenging, suggest that the children follow the scent trail with their eyes closed.

Glue magnet to craft stick

Glue paper clip on back of ant

SONGS AND ACTIVITIES

## Book Corner

### Language/Math

❍ Photocopy the Ants Go Marching Rhyme Cards (page 111). Color them, cut them out, and laminate them. Have the children match each numeral in the song to the correct rhyming word card.

### Math

❍ Cut 1" x 12" strips of paper. Draw trails of ants on each strip, starting with a trail of one ant on the first strip, two ants on the second strip, and so on up to eight ants. Have the children arrange them from the strip with the least ants to the strip with the most ants.

✓ **Special Needs Adaptation:** Talk about how ants work together in groups and help each other. Ask for a volunteer to help the child with special needs complete this math activity (and any of the other activities). Talk about the importance of working together.

### Movement

❍ Encourage the children to march in a line as if they are ants.

### Outdoors

❍ Place a spoonful of sugar outdoors near a place where there are anthills or where you have seen ants. Invite the children to watch the ants carry the sugar back to their homes.

### Snack

❍ Serve Ants on a Log for snack. Invite the children to fill the hollow side of a four-inch strip of celery with peanut butter to create a log and raisins for them to use for ants. **Allergy Note:** If any of the children have peanut allergies, substitute cream cheese for peanut butter.

# Home Connection

❍ Encourage children to ask their families to help them look outside their homes for anthills. Remind the children not to disturb the anthills.

# The Insect Song

## Vocabulary

insect
head
thorax
abdomen
legs
wings
antennae

## Theme Connections

Counting
Parts of the Body

(Tune: Head, Shoulders, Knees, and Toes)
Head, thorax, abdomen,
Abdomen.
Head, thorax, abdomen,
Abdomen.
Six legs, four wings, antennae two
Head, thorax, abdomen,
Abdomen.

 **English Language Learner Strategy:** Hold a photo of an insect while singing the song. Point to the parts of the insect's body as you sing.

## Did You Know?

○ There are well over one million known species of insects in the world, and some experts estimate that there might be as many as ten million.

○ All insects must have three body parts: a head, a thorax, and an abdomen; six jointed legs; two antennae to sense the world around them; and an exoskeleton (outside skeleton). If all four of these things are not present, then it is not an insect! Spiders are not insects because they have eight legs and do not have three body parts. Centipedes and millipedes have way too many legs to be insects! Most insects have one or two pairs of wings, but wings are not necessary for classification as an insect.

○ A cockroach can live for nine days without its head.

○ Dragonflies can fly at speeds up to 30 miles per hour.

○ The color a head louse will be as an adult depends on the color of the person's hair in which it lives.

## Literacy Links

### Comprehension

○ Sing the song and then sing "Head, Shoulders, Knees, and Toes." Encourage the children to compare insect body parts to human body parts. *What part of our body do we call our abdomen?* (The more

common term is *stomach* or *tummy*.) *Do humans have antennae? Insects use their antennae to hear sounds. What do humans use to hear sounds?*

### Oral Language

○ Talk about insects. Explain that all insects have three body parts, six legs, two antennae, and an outer skeleton. Point out that spiders are not insects. Check their characteristics using the Rebus Insect Checklist (page 118).

○ Teach the children the American Sign Language sign for *insect* and *bug* (page 121).

# Curriculum Connections

### Art

○ Provide crayons and paper and encourage the children to draw a picture of their favorite insect.

> **Special Needs Adaptation:** Adapt a pencil or crayon for children with motor difficulties by wrapping several layers of tape around it. This will enable the child to use the pencil or crayon more easily. Grips can also be made with foam hair rollers. These can be purchased in packages of 12. Remove the center plastic and insert the crayon into the foam roller.

### Fine Motor

○ Photocopy and enlarge the insects from the Bug Pattern Cards (pages 105-106). Color each insect, cut it out, and laminate it. Cut the insects into puzzle pieces. Make a different colored mark on pieces of each puzzle so the pieces do not get mixed up.

○ Provide playdough and pipe cleaners. Invite the children to make insects using the pipe cleaners for antennae and legs.

**Book Corner**

*Bugs Are Insects* by
Anne Rockwell
*On Beyond Bugs: All
About Insects* by
Tish Rabe
*What Is an Insect?* by
Susan Canizares

### Games

○ Make two photocopies of the Bug Pattern Cards (pages 105-106). Color them, cut them out, and laminate them. Invite the children to play a concentration game with the Bug Pattern Cards.

### Movement

○ Have the children move like insects: fly like a bee, hop like a grasshopper, scurry like an ant, (hover) in the air like a mosquito, and so on.

✓ **English Language Learner Strategy:** Show a picture of a fly, grasshopper, ant, or mosquito and then model the corresponding movement. Suggest that the child mimic your actions. Say the name of the insect and describe the action.

### Outdoors

○ Have children choose a partner. Give each pair of children a 36″ strip of yarn. Instruct them to make a circle on the ground with their yarn. Then give each pair of children a magnifying glass and ask them to search inside their circle for bugs. Do they find any insects or bugs?

### Science

○ Provide pictures of insects and other bugs. Encourage the children to sort the bugs into two categories: insect and not an insect. Photocopy the Rebus Insect Checklist (page 118). Color it and laminate it. Provide it as a checklist so children can check their sorting. Help the children as needed.

### Social Studies

○ Help the children brainstorm a list of ways that insects are helpful to humans; for example, ladybugs eat other insects that are harmful to crops, bees pollinate flowers (carry the pollen from one flower to another flower) and produce honey, and many insects aid in the decomposition of trash.

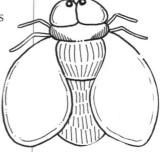

# Home Connection

○ Suggest that children ask their families to participate in an insect hunt outdoors. Have them keep count of how many different insects they find. Invite them to report their findings at school. Who found the most insects?

# My Pet Mosquito

I once had a little pet mosquito.
She loved to go outside and play.
But when my friends saw my pet mosquito,
They slapped her and scared her away.

✓ **Special Needs Adaptation:** Talk about where mosquitoes live and where they are likely to be found. Reinforce your discussion with pictures.

## Vocabulary

mosquito
outside
pet
play
scared
slapped

## Theme Connections

Friends and Families
Pets

## Did You Know?

○ The heat from a person's body enhances a mosquito's vision, making it easier for mosquitoes to find us!

○ Adult mosquitoes feed on carbohydrate (sugar) sources, such as nectar and fruit juice.

○ Most mosquitoes stay within one mile of their breeding site.

○ In the United States, mosquitoes are responsible for diseases such as encephalitis, malaria, and dog heartworm. Worldwide, mosquito-borne diseases kill more people than any other disease.

○ See page 19 in "Mosquitoes" and page 82 in "Flea Fly Flow Mosquito" for additional information about mosquitoes.

## Literacy Links

### Oral Language

○ Encourage children to talk about bugs they have captured for pets. Remind them to let any bugs go after a few hours of observation. Ask them to describe a bug they would like to have for a temporary "pet."

○ Discuss other ways the mosquito in the song could have been frightened away besides being slapped. **Note:** Talk about the importance of being gentle with other people and with animals.

○ Teach the children the American Sign Language sign for *mosquito* (page 122).

### Print Awareness

○ Encourage the children to brainstorm a list of names for a pet mosquito. If they need help getting started, offer a few suggestions, such as *Pesky* or *Bitey.* Print the names on chart paper. Have the children review the list and vote on a favorite name.

### Segmentation

○ Ask the children to slap their legs gently to mark the number of syllables in *mosquito.* Challenge them to find a friend who has a name with the same number of syllables as *mosquito.*

# Curriculum Connections

### Art

○ Invite the children to draw a picture of a pet they would like to have.

### Blocks

○ Provide boxes, plastic berry baskets, tubes, and other materials so the children can build a home for a pet mosquito. *Where will the mosquito sleep? What will he eat?*

### Discovery

○ Use the Mosquito Life Span Sequence Cards (pages 112-114) to discuss the life cycle of the mosquito. First, the female mosquito drops her eggs into water. A *wriggler* hatches from each egg. It eats tiny animals in the water. In a week, the wriggler changes into a *pupa,* which floats just under the water. In a few days the pupa's skin splits down the back and a *winged adult mosquito* comes out. Challenge the children to sequence the cards.

 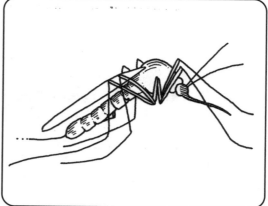

## Book Corner

*Can I Keep Him?* by
 Steven Kellogg
*Mosquito* by Jennifer
 Coldrey
*The Perfect Pet* by
 Margie Palatini

### Games

❍ Make two photocopies of the Bug Pattern Cards (pages 105-106). Color the cards, cut them out, and laminate them. Separate the insect cards from the bug cards. Encourage the children to play Bug Concentration.

### Science

❍ Show the children a photo of a mosquito. Photocopy and laminate the Rebus Insect Checklist (page 118). Encourage the children to check the list to see if the mosquito is a true insect with three body parts, two antennae, six legs, and an outer skeleton.

### Snack

❍ Provide straws and invite the children to drink their juice like a mosquito drinks its dinner. Slurp!

### Writing

❍ Print *mosquito* on index cards. Invite the children to cover the lines of the letters with red dots (representing mosquito bites) by using the tip of red markers.

❍ See additional activities for mosquitoes on pages 19-21 in "Mosquitoes" and pages 82-84 in "Flea Fly Flow Mosquito."

# Home Connection

❍ Encourage the children to ask their families what they have in the medicine cabinet to ease the discomfort of a mosquito bite.

# Nobody Likes Me

## Vocabulary

fat
first
fuzzy
germ
hate
juicy
like
long
second
short
skinny
slim
slimy
squirm
thin
wiggle
worm

## Theme Connections

Feelings
Friends and Families

Nobody likes me, everybody hates me,
Guess I'll go eat worms.
Long, thin, slimy ones;
Short, fat, juicy ones,
Itsy, bitsy, fuzzy, wuzzy worms.

Down goes the first one, down goes the second one,
Oh, how they wiggle and squirm.
Up comes the first one,
Up comes the second one,
Oh, how they wiggle and squirm.

Nobody likes me, everybody hates me,
Think I'll go eat worms.
Big, fat, juicy ones;
Little, slimy, skinny ones;
Hope they don't have germs!

✓ **Special Needs Adaptation:** It is very important to explain that this is a pretend song. Many children with special needs, especially those with cognitive challenges, are very literal. If you sing a song about eating worms, they may assume that it is okay to eat worms. Talk about the importance of never putting anything in -their mouths without first asking an adult. Explain that some insects, plants, and substances can be very harmful when swallowed. Tell the children that eating any bug or insect is not ever a good idea.

## Did You Know?

○ There are approximately 2,700 kinds of earthworms.
○ A worm does not have arms, legs, or eyes. Although worms do not have eyes, they can sense light, especially at their anterior or front end. They move away from light and will become paralyzed if exposed to light for more than one hour.
○ Worms live where there is food, moisture, oxygen, and a favorable temperature because they are cold-blooded animals. If a worm's skin dries out, the worm will die.
○ Worms can grow a new tail if their tails are cut off.

# Literacy Links

### Letter Knowledge
❍ Print *fuzzy wuzzy* on chart paper. Ask the children to find the letter in each word that does not appear in the other word. Have them identify the letters in each word.

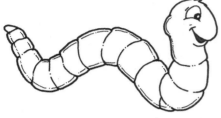

### Oral Language
❍ Discuss worms and caterpillars. *How are they alike? How are they different?* Make a Venn Diagram (page 119) to show likenesses and differences.
❍ Discuss the adjectives used in the song to describe the worms, such as *long, skinny, slimy, fat, short*, and so on.
❍ Teach the children the American Sign Language sign for *worm* (page 122).

### Phonological Awareness
❍ Print *fuzzy wuzzy* on chart paper. Say the words several times. Point out that the words rhyme. Discuss other words that rhyme with *fuzzy* and *wuzzy*. At another time, try the same activity using *itsy bitsy*.

# Curriculum Connections

### Art
❍ Provide brown and grey tempera paint. Invite the children to paint pictures of worms.

### Construction

❍ Let each child paint six or eight tin cans. Cover the perimeter of the open tops with duct tape beforehand to protect the children from rough edges. Poke a hole in the bottom of each can (adult only) and have children string the cans together to make a worm. Have them paint a face on the end can.

### Fine Motor
❍ Provide brown and grey playdough. Encourage the children to roll it into worms. Have them make fat worms, skinny worms, long worms, and short worms. *Can you make your worms wiggle and squirm?*

## Gross Motor

○ Invite the children to lie on the floor face down and wiggle like worms. Make a start and finish line and challenge them to wiggle from one line to the next. Make sure they know they can't use their arms and legs. *Why is it so hard to move?*

## Math

○ Cut fuzzy yarn into 6" strips to represent worms. Have the children use the yarn "worms" to measure things in the room. *Can you find a block that is the same length as the worm? Can you find a book that is same length as two worms?*

○ Cut strips of plastic laces or string into 1", 2", 3", 4", and 5" lengths. Challenge the children to arrange the "worms" from shortest to longest horizontally and then vertically.

## Music

○ Teach the children "Can You Wiggle, Squiggle, Squirm?" to the tune of "Do Your Ears Hang Low?"

> **Can You Wiggle, Squiggle, Squirm?**
> *Can you wiggle like a worm?*
> *Can you squiggle, can you squirm?*
> *Can you waggle when you wiggle?*
> *Does it all make you giggle?*
> *Can you wiggle, woggle, waggle?*
> *Can you squiggle, squoggle, squaggle?*
> *Can you wiggle like a worm?*

## Outdoors

○ Dig a shallow hole outdoors in a garden or flower bed. Invite the children to observe the worms working just below the surface. Make sure not to leave the worms exposed to the air and sun for too long. They are vulnerable when exposed to air.

## Snack

○ Invite the children to follow the Cup of Worms Rebus (page 100) to make a snack.

 **English Language Learner Strategy:** Using a rebus makes it easier for English language learners to follow the directions.

## Book Corner

*Beetle McGrady Eats Bugs!* by Megan McDonald
*Grandpas Are for Finding Worms* by Harriet Ziefert
*Wonderful Worms* by Linda Glaser

NOBODY LIKES ME

### Cup of Worms

Place 2 tablespoons of Cool Whip in a small plastic cup.

Crumble one chocolate cookie and place the crumbs on top of the Cool Whip.

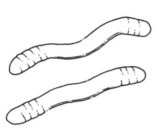 

Add 2 gummy worms.

Eat the cup of worms!

### Writing

○ Print *fuzzy wuzzy* on drawing paper. Provide squeeze bottles of glue and have the children trace over the letters with the glue. Provide fuzzy pieces of yarn to put on top of the glue to make *fuzzy wuzzy* letters.

○ Print the names of several insects, such as *bee, ant, fly, mosquito,* and *flea,* on index cards. Encourage the children to use magnetic letters to copy the insect names.

# Home Connection

○ Encourage the children to ask their families to help them look in flower beds or flower pots for worms. Remind the children to tell their families that the presence of worms means that the soil is healthy. Remind them to bury the worms back in the earth after finding them.

# Fuzzy Caterpillar

## Vocabulary

butterfly
caterpillar
crawl
disappointed
fuzzy
metamorphosis
pretty
tear
town
walk
worm

A fuzzy caterpillar went out for a walk.
His back went up and down.
He crawled and he crawled
And he crawled and he crawled
'Til he crawled all over town.
He wasn't disappointed
Not a bit to be a worm.
Not a tear was in his eye.
Because he knew that he would become
A very, very pretty butterfly.

## Theme Connections

Movement
Spatial Relationships

## Did You Know?

### Caterpillars

○ A caterpillar grows to about 27,000 times the size it was when it first emerged from its egg. If a human baby weighed 9 pounds at birth and grew at the same rate as a caterpillar, it would weigh 243,000 pounds when fully grown!

○ Because the caterpillar's skin does not grow along with it as human skin does, it must shed the skin periodically as it becomes too tight. This is called *molting*.

### Butterflies

○ There are some 24,000 species of butterflies. Butterflies range in size from a tiny ⅛ inch to almost 12 inches.

○ Butterflies can see the colors red, green, and yellow.

○ Butterflies taste with their feet! Their taste sensors are located in the feet; by standing on their food, they can taste it! All butterflies have six legs and six feet. In some species such as the *monarch*, the front pair of legs remains tucked up under the body most of the time and is difficult to see.

○ Butterfly wings are transparent. The iridescent scales, which overlap like shingles on a roof, give the wings the colors we see.

○ See page 62 for more information about caterpillars and butterflies.

# Literacy Links

### Comprehension

❍ Encourage children to sequence the stages of metamorphosis. Purchase a green sock or dye a white sock green. Glue wiggle eyes and a red felt mouth on one side of the sock to make a caterpillar. Turn the sock inside out and glue wiggle eyes, a red felt mouth, antennae, and felt wings to make a butterfly. Use the puppet to show the transformation of a caterpillar into a butterfly. Teach the children the action rhyme, "Metamorphosis" (page 63).

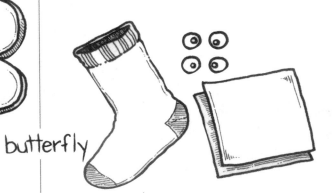
butterfly

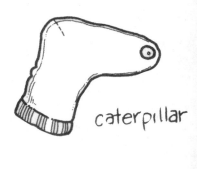
caterpillar

❍ Print *butterfly* on chart paper. Draw a line between *butter* and *fly*. Point out that *butterfly* is made up of two words. Explain that when a word is made up of two words it is called a *compound word*.

✔ **Special Needs Adaptation:** For children who have cognitive challenges, after explaining that butter and fly make up the compound word butterfly, look for other compound words to explain the concept, such as *baseball, cupcake, outdoor,* and *beanbag.*

### Oral Language

❍ Teach the children the American Sign Language signs for *caterpillar* and *butterfly* (page 121).

### Oral Language/Print Awareness

❍ Discuss the differences between a butterfly and a caterpillar. *Are they both insects?* Check their body parts with the Rebus Insect Checklist (page 118).

# Curriculum Connections

### Art

○ Give each child a sheet of construction paper. Show them how to fold their paper in half. Drop a spoon of thick liquid tempera paint on one side of the fold. Have the children fold their paper and then press over the sheet of paper. When they open the paper they will have a beautiful butterfly.

### Discovery

○ Mix dry yellow tempera paint with powder to create a substance that looks like pollen. Provide pipe cleaners. Show the children how to dip a pipe cleaner in the "pollen" and then rub a second pipe cleaner over it to release the "pollen." Point out to the children that one way butterflies carry pollen from one flower to the next is by catching it on their legs and then rubbing their legs together to drop the pollen on a second flower.

### Gross Motor

○ Place a long and wavy masking tape line on the floor and encourage the children to crawl along it like a caterpillar.

### Language

○ Give the children the puppet used in the literacy link. Encourage them to use the puppet to act out the sequences of metamorphosis.

### Math

○ Cut thick yarn into 2" strips to represent caterpillars. Print one numeral, one through five, in the center of each paper plate. Invite the children to count the appropriate number of caterpillars onto each plate.

### Music and Movement

○ Give each child two paper plates. Provide crayons and paint and invite the children to decorate their plates to look like butterfly wings. Let dry. Play classical music and encourage the children to use their wings to fly like butterflies.

✓ **Special Needs Adaptation:** For children with physical challenges, after the child decorates her paper plate wings, use a hole punch to punch two holes in each plate. The holes should be about three inches apart. Place a piece of ribbon or yarn through each hole and tie it gently to the child's hand.

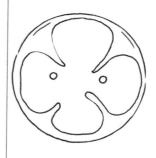
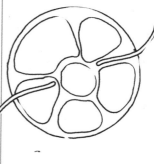

## Book Corner

*Bubba and Trixie* by Lisa Campbell Ernst

*Clara Caterpillar* by Pamela Duncan Edwards

*From Caterpillar to Butterfly* by Deborah Heiligman

*Monarch Butterfly* by Gail Gibbons

*Where Butterflies Grow* by Joanne Ryder

### Outdoors

○ Plant milkweed around the perimeter of the playground. Butterflies love milkweed. They will come to eat and lay their eggs there. The eggs will hatch into caterpillars, and you will be able to observe the entire life cycle of the butterfly.

### Science

○ Photocopy the Metamorphosis Sequence Cards (page 115). Color them, cut them out, and laminate them. Invite the children to sequence the cards.

○ Provide a photo of a caterpillar and a butterfly. Challenge children to use the Rebus Insect Checklist (page 118) to determine if the caterpillar and the butterfly are insects. *Does the caterpillar have three body parts, two antennae, six legs, and an outer skeleton? Does the butterfly have three body parts, two antennae, six legs, and an outer skeleton?*

# Home Connection

○ Suggest that the children show their families how caterpillars move.

# Little Ant's Hill/ Little Bee's Hive

## Vocabulary

alive
ant
anthill
bee
beehive
foot
hill
off
ouch
remove
still

Oh, I stuck my foot
On a little ant's hill,
And the little ant said,
"You better be still,
Take it off! Take it off!
Take it off! Remove it!"

Oh, I didn't take it off,
And the little ant said,
"If you don't take it off
You'll wish you had.
Take it off! Take it off!"
Ouch! I removed it!

Oh, I stuck my hand
In a little bee's hive,
And the little bee said,
"Goodness, alive!
Take it out! Take it out!
Take it out! Remove it!"

Oh, I didn't take it out,
And the little bee said,
"If you don't take it out
You'll wish you had.
Take it out! Take it out!"
Buzzz! I removed it!

## Theme Connections

Animals
Health and Safety
Sounds

## Did You Know?

### Ants

❍ Worker ants are sterile. They look for food, care for their young, and defend the nest (anthill) from unwanted visitors. Ants are clean and tidy insects. Some worker ants are given the job of taking the rubbish from the nest and putting it outside in a special rubbish dump!

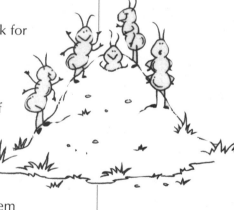

❍ Worker ants keep the eggs and larvae in different groups, according to age. At night, worker ants move the colony's eggs and larvae deep into the nest to protect them from the cold. During the daytime, the worker ants move the colony's eggs and larvae to the top of the nest so that they can be warmer.

❍ If a worker ant has found a good source for food, it leaves a trail of scent so the other ants in the colony can find the food.

### Bees

❍ Bees live in large groups called *colonies*. Their dwellings are called *hives*. The leader of each hive is the *queen*. She directs the activities of the workers and the drones.

○ The honeybee pollinates plants, which helps the farming industry in the production of crops. Pollination also helps the spread of wild plants.
○ Bees are the only insects that make a food—honey—that humans eat. Beeswax is used in making soap, furniture polish, candles, and many other products.
○ See page 16 in "Baby Bumblebee," page 22 in "The Ants Go Marching," page 59 in "Little Ants," and page 94 for additional information about bees and ants.

# Literacy Links

### Comprehension
○ Print *anthill* and *beehive* on chart paper. Draw a line between *ant* and *hill* and *bee* and *hive*. Point out that *bee* and *hive* and *ant* and *hill* are each words. Explain that when two words are put together to make a new word, the new word is called a *compound word*.
○ Challenge the children to think of a word that describes an ant, and then to think of a word that describes a bee.

### Listening
○ Have the children stand up each time they hear *ant* and each time they hear *bee*.

> **Special Needs Adaptation:** Modify this activity for children with cognitive challenges by making two flash cards. On one flashcard, glue or draw a large ant and write ant below the picture. Do the same with a picture of a bee. When you say ant, hold up the card as a cue for the child to stand up; when you say bee, do the same thing with the other card. These visual cues help the child know what you want him to do. It may be necessary to model the activity once or twice with a peer volunteer, so the child understands exactly how to do the activity.

### Oral Language
○ Discuss honey. Talk about pollination. Ask the children why they think honey is a golden color.
○ Teach the children the American Sign Language sign for *bee* and *ant* (page 121).

**Phonological Awareness**
- ○ Challenge the children to think of other words that rhyme with *hill* and *still* and then with *hive* and *alive*.

# Curriculum Connections

### Art
- ○ Provide yellow and black tempera paint. Have the children paint yellow and black stripes.

### Construction
- ○ Cut out each of the twelve bottom sections of a number of egg cartons (each carton will have 12 bottom sections). Give the children glue, gold paint, and the bottom sections of egg cartons. Encourage them to construct a honeycomb. If possible, display a real honeycomb.

### Discovery
- ○ Place an ant farm in the science center for observation.

### Fine Motor
- ○ Provide clay and toothpicks. Encourage the children to shape anthills and use the toothpicks to make tunnels.

### Math
- ○ Provide yellow and black strips of construction paper. Invite the children to lay the strips in a pattern of black and yellow. Show them variations in patterns; for example, two yellow strips, one black strip, two yellow strips, one black strip, and so on.

### Outdoors
- ○ Ants can teach us how some insects work together as a community. Watch ants scurry in and out of their anthills, or spill some dry cereal on the sidewalk and see what the ants do. *Do they eat their food on the spot or carry it back to their anthill?* When an ant finds food, it runs back to the hill to "tell" the other ants. As it runs, the ant leaves a trail of scent the other ants can smell. The other ants find the food by smelling their way along the trail.

### Sand Table
- ○ Encourage the children to build anthills. If possible, provide plastic ants to live in the anthills.

## Book Corner

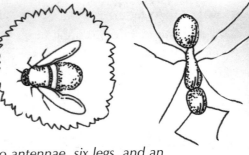

### Science

○ Provide a photo of a bee and an ant. Challenge the children to use the Rebus Insect Checklist (page 118) to determine if the bee and the ant are insects. *Does the ant have three body parts, two antennae, six legs, and an outer skeleton? Does the bee have three body parts, two antennae, six legs, and an outer skeleton?*

### Snack

○ Provide honey. Invite the children to try a little honey on a piece of toast.

### Writing

○ Mix dry yellow tempera paint with powder to make pretend pollen. Spread the pollen on the bottom of meat trays. Provide toothpicks. Encourage the children to use the toothpicks to write in *bee* in the pollen.

○ See pages 16-18 in "Baby Bumblebee," pages 59-61 in "Little Ants," and Pages 22-24 in "The Ants Go Marching" for additional activities about bees and ants.

# Home Connection

○ Teach the children "The Beehive" (page 93). Suggest that children teach the fingerplay to their families.

# Bugs

## Vocabulary

big
chirp
crawl
creep
falling
loud
night
quiet
sing
small
zing

(Tune: Are You Sleeping?)
Big bugs, small bugs, big bugs, small bugs,
See them crawl up the wall.
Creeping and a-crawling,
How do they keep from falling?
Bug, bugs, bugs, bugs, bugs, bugs.

Quiet bugs, loud bugs, quiet bugs, loud bugs,
Hear them sing in the night.
Chirping and a-zinging,
All through the night they're singing.
Bugs, bugs, bugs, bugs, bugs, bugs.

## Theme Connections

Movement
Nighttime
Opposites
Sounds

## Did You Know?

○ All insects must have three body parts (a head, a thorax, and an abdomen), six jointed legs, two antennae to sense the world around them, and an exoskeleton (outside skeleton). If all four are not found, it cannot be called an insect! Spiders are not insects because they have eight legs and do not have three body parts. Centipedes and millipedes have way too many legs to be called insects!

○ Many insects have one or two pairs of wings, but wings are not necessary for classification as an insect.

# Literacy Links

### Comprehension
○ Invite a volunteer to demonstrate creeping and crawling.

### Oral Language
○ Discuss the difference between insects and bugs. Have the children name some big bugs and some small bugs.
○ Teach the children the American Sign Language sign for *bug* (page 121).

### Phonological Awareness

○ Invite the children to brainstorm a list of words that rhyme with *bug*.

### Print Awareness

○ Print the song on chart paper. Move your hand under the words as you sing the song. Point out the left-to-right and top-to-bottom direction of the print.

# Curriculum Connections

### Art

○ Provide paint and brushes. Invite the children to splatter the paint onto paper and then determine if the splatter looks like a bug. *If the splatter looks like a bug, which bug does it look like?*

### Construction

○ Provide boxes, pipe cleaners, wiggle eyes, tempera paint, and egg cartons. Invite the children to construct bugs.

○ Make Crazy Bug Hats. Provide the children with pipe cleaners, pompom balls, construction paper, glue, staplers, feathers, beads, markers, and other materials to make Crazy Bug Hats. Challenge the children to make up a bug name for themselves. When everyone is finished, have a bug fashion show. Introduce each "bug" by name and have her walk in front of the other children.

 **Special Needs Adaptation:**
Provide additional support to children who have physical limitations by giving them tongs to pick up the items and using larger materials that are easier to hold. Use glue that they do not have to touch, such as glue sticks, and large pipe cleaners. This activity offers an excellent opportunity to work together in pairs just like insects. This helps the children learn important social skills and encourages a sense of collaboration.

## Fine Motor

○ Photocopy and enlarge the bugs from the Bug Pattern Cards (page 106). Color them, cut them out, and laminate them. Cut the cards into puzzle pieces. Use a colored marker to mark the back of the puzzle pieces for each bug so that they do not get mixed up. Invite the children to work the puzzles.

## Games

○ Make two photocopies of the Bug Pattern Cards (page 106). Color them, cut them out, and laminate them. Encourage the children to play Bug Concentration.

**Special Needs Adaptation:** Enlarge the photocopies of the Bug Pattern Cards. For children who might have difficulty with Bug Concentration, start by asking them to match the cards to each other. If you introduce the idea of a concentration game, start with two pairs of cards. As the child begins to understand how the game is played, add more cards. Don't forget to model the game before you play it with the child.

## Math

○ Invite the children to fold a piece of paper in half. Then the children place their fingers on a stamp pad and use their inked fingers to make fingerprint bugs on each half of their paper. When they have finished, have them count the bugs on each half of their paper.

## Music

○ Sing "There Was an Old Lady Who Swallowed a Fly." Discuss which animals mentioned in the song are insects, which are bugs, and which are neither.

## Science

○ Provide photos of bugs. Invite children to sort the photos by size: bugs that are large and bugs that are small. When they have finished sorting by size, have the children sort the bugs by those that are loud and those that are quiet.

## Book Corner

*The Best Book of Bugs* by Claire Llewellyn

*I Like Bugs* by Margaret Wise Brown

*The Icky Bug Alphabet Book* by Jerry Pallotta

### Social Studies

○ Help children think about ways bugs help people. Make a list of ways people can be kinder to bugs; for example, leaving them in their natural habitat and not harming them. Be sure to emphasize that all living things play a role in making the earth a good place to live.

### Writing

○ Print the names of insects and bugs on index cards. Invite the children to trace over the bug names using tracing paper and crayons.

# Home Connection

○ Ask families to send live nonpoisonous insects or dead specimens to school in a clear jar with a lid with holes punched in it to allow live insects to breathe. Provide magnifying glasses so children can have a close-up look of the insects and bugs. Discuss the number of legs, wings, and antennae on each insect. Encourage the children to compare the bugs. At the end of the day, let the live bugs return to nature.

# Grasshopper

## Vocabulary

back
bumblebee
busy
down
first
flea
flew
flu
fly
grasshopper
jump
leapfrog
second
spider

## Theme Connections

Humor
Movement
Spatial Relationships

((Tune: Battle Hymn of the Republic)
The first grasshopper jumped right over
The second grasshopper's back.
Oh, the first grasshopper jumped right over
The second grasshopper's back.
The first grasshopper jumped right over
The second grasshopper's back.
Oh, the first grasshopper jumped right over
The second grasshopper's back.

They were only playing leapfrog!
They were only playing leapfrog!
They were only playing leapfrog!
When the first grasshopper jumped right over
The second grasshopper's back.

As one busy buzzing bumblebee
Was busily buzzing by. *(repeat three more times)*

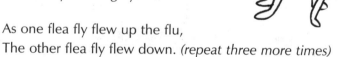

They were only playing leapfrog!
They were only playing leapfrog!
They were only playing leapfrog!
As one busy buzzing bumblebee
Was busily buzzing by.

As one flea fly flew up the flu,
The other flea fly flew down. *(repeat three more times)*

They were only playing leapfrog!
They were only playing leapfrog!
They were only playing leapfrog!
As one flea fly flew up the flu,
The other flea fly flew down.

A spider spied a spider on
Another spider's back. *(repeat three more times)*

They were only playing leapfrog!
They were only playing leapfrog!
They were only playing leapfrog!
As a spider spied a spider on
Another spider's back.

# Did You Know?

**Grasshoppers**

❍ Grasshoppers can be found almost everywhere in the world, except for the colder regions near the North and South Poles. They live in fields, meadows, and just about anywhere they can find generous amounts of leaves to eat.

❍ Grasshoppers have five eyes and no ears, and they hear through their legs. Grasshoppers have two sets of wings.

**Fleas**

❍ Fleas have been around for about 100 million years. They lived with the dinosaurs!

❍ Some fleas can jump 150 times their own length, which is comparable to a person jumping 1,000 feet. One flea broke a record with a four-foot vertical jump.

**Spiders**

❍ Spiders have eight eyes, eight legs, two body parts, outside skeletons, and fangs. They do not have antennas or wings. Male spiders are smaller than females.

❍ See information about bees in "Baby Bumblebee" on page 16, in "The Pup and the Bee" on page 51, in "Little Ant's Hill" on page 39, and on page 94.

# Literacy Links

## Comprehension

❍ Print *grasshopper* and *leapfrog* on chart paper. Draw a line between *grass* and *hopper* and between *leap* and *frog*. Point out that each of these words is made up of two words. Explain that when a word is made up of two words that could each stand alone it is called a *compound word*. Ask the children to brainstorm other compound words, such as *doghouse* and *popcorn*.

## Comprehension/Oral Language

❍ Print *grasshopper* on chart paper and draw a circle around the word. Encourage the children to tell you what they know about grasshoppers. Print the information they share on lines that extend out from the circled word. At another time, do the same for bees, spiders, and fleas.

**Phonological Awareness**

○   Point out the *alliterative phrases* (repetition of beginning sounds in a series of words) in the song. Ask volunteers to reproduce the sounds they hear repeated.

# Curriculum Connections

## Games

○   Teach the children how to play Leapfrog. Select one child to be "the frog." Ask the other children to get on the floor on their hands and knees and crouch down. Invite the frog to leap over the children by placing her hands on the back of each child for support while she straddles her legs around their body and hops over them. **Safety Note:** Supervise this activity closely and assist children as they leap.

## Gross Motor

○   Discuss the movements of grasshoppers and fleas. Tell the children that when jumping insects move, they use a catapulting motion, like people when they bounce and jump. Invite the children to try the bounce and jump movement.

○   Make Grasshopper Hoppers by spraying ping-pong balls with green paint (away from the children) and then using a felt tip pen to draw eyes on them. Have the children try to make the "grasshoppers" hop by bouncing them on the floor. Challenge them to make the Grasshopper Hoppers bounce once and then land in a box.

## Book Corner

### Listening
○ Invite the children to rub a craft stick across the teeth of a plastic comb to simulate the sounds grasshoppers make when they rub their legs together.

### Math
○ Give the children 3" pieces of yarn that represent the length of a large grasshopper. Encourage the children to locate things in the classroom that are the size of a large grasshopper.

> ✓ **Special Needs Adaptation:** For children with cognitive challenges, start by giving them a length of yarn. Model how to measure with it. Provide two shoeboxes and four items that are the same size as the length of yarn, and two that are longer. Help the child measure each item. Show him how to place items that are the same size as the yarn in one box and the items that are not the same size in the other box.

### Music
○ Play some peppy music and invite the children to hop like fleas.

### Outdoors
○ Show the children how to take a few steps and then bounce and jump. Place a piece of rope on the ground as a jump line. Invite the children to take a few running steps, bounce on the start line, and then jump. Measure the distance of their jumps.

### Science
○ Provide photos of a grasshopper, a flea, and a spider. Photocopy the Rebus Insect Checklist (page 118). Encourage the children to use the checklist to determine if the grasshopper, flea, and spider are insects or bugs.

○ See pages 16-18 and 51-54 for additional activities about bees.

# Home Connection

○ Encourage the children to show family members how to play Leapfrog.

# The Bee and the Pup

## Vocabulary

bee        sat
buzz      wall
pup

## Theme Connections

Animals
Sounds

There was a bee-i-ee-i-ee
Sat on a wall-i-all-i-all,
And he went buzz-i-uzz-i-uzz
And that was all-i-all-i-all.
There was a pup-i-up-i-up
Sat on that bee-i-ee-i-ee,
And he went i-yi-yi-yi-yi
And that was he-he-he-he-he.
HA HA!

## Did You Know?

○ Bees like to nest in wooden storage sheds, small barns, and garages.

○ Bumblebees are common, inconspicuous insects. Inside the nest of bumblebees lives a colony of social insects that may number 200 or more. Members engage in most of the activities of a human society—gathering food, caring for offspring, constructing a home, and defending and regulating their home environment.

○ Bumblebees have very few natural enemies. Skunks are one of the few animals that find bumblebees tasty, sting and all.

○ For information about how to avoid bee stings, see page 95.

○ See page 16 in "Baby Bumblebee" for more information about bees.

## Literacy Links

### Letter Knowledge

○ Print the first stanza of the song on chart paper. Show the children places in the song where letters are used instead of words. Encourage the children to name the letters. Sing the song together.

### Listening

○ Have the children stand up and sit down every time they hear the sound /ee/.

### Oral Language

○ Discuss bees with the children. *Who has seen a bee? Where did you see the bee? What was it doing? Has anyone been stung by a bee? How did it happen? What can you do to keep from being stung? What should you do if you get stung?*

○ Teach the children the American Sign Language sign for *bee* and for *pup* (page 121). Sing the song using the signs where they belong.

### Phonological Awareness

○ Sing this alternate version of the song. Ask the children how the last line would sound if the celebration word was "hooray" instead of "yippee."

> *There was a bug-i-ug-i-ug*
> *Sat on a stone-i-one-i-one,*
> *And he went buzz-i-uzz-i-uzz*
> *He was alone, alone, alone.*
> *Another bug-i-ug-i-ug*
> *Crawled on that stone-i-one-i-one,*
> *And now there's two-i-oo-i-oo*
> *He's not alone, alone, alone.*
> *Yippee!*

# Curriculum Connections

### Blocks

○ Provide a plastic dog and a yellow pompom to represent a bee. Have the children build a wall and re-enact the song.

### Fine Motor

○ Make and enlarge two or three photocopies of the bee from the Bug Pattern Card (page 105). Color them, cut them out, laminate them, and cut them into puzzle pieces. Use colored markers to make marks on the back of puzzle pieces so the individual puzzle pieces do not get mixed up. Challenge the children to work the puzzles.

○ Photocopy the bee from the Bug Pattern Cards (page 105). Color it, cut it out, laminate it, and glue a paper clip to the back of it. Draw a path that goes from a flower to a wall on a 9" x 12"

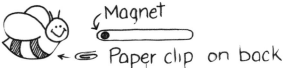

Magnet

Paper clip on back

sheet of poster board. Place the bee on the pathway near the flower. Show children how to move a large magnet under the poster board to move the bee from the flower to the wall.

## Games

❍ Invite the children to play Dog and Bee the way you would play Dog and Bone. Children sit in a circle. One child—IT—walks around the outside of the circle, carrying a paper or plastic bee. Eventually IT drops the bee behind a player. That player picks up the bee and chases IT around the circle. If she taps IT before IT gets around the circle, IT goes to the "beehive" (the center of the circle). If she does not, IT takes her place in the circle. The player with the bee becomes the new IT as the game continues.

## Language

❍ Photocopy the bee from the Bug Pattern Cards (page 105). Color it, cut it out, laminate it, and glue a tongue depressor to create a Bee Puppet. Decorate a paper cup to look like a brick wall. Cut a slit in the bottom of the cup and stick the tongue depressor through the slit. Show the children how to move the bee puppet from behind the wall to the top of the wall.

## Math

❍ Provide pollen made from yellow tempera paint and powder, a small spoon, and paper plates numbered from 1-5. Challenge children to place the number of spoons of pollen as indicated by the numeral on the plate.

**Special Needs Adaptation:** Use cutouts of bees instead of pollen. Encourage the child to put the number of bees in each plate that correspond to the number written on the plate. Children with autism spectrum disorder and/or cognitive challenges will find this adaptation more concrete and easier to understand than the spoons and the pretend pollen.

## Science

❍ Provide a picture of a bee. Photocopy and laminate the Rebus Insect Checklist (page 118). Encourage the children to check the list to see if the bee is a true insect—three body parts, two antennae, six legs, and an outer skeleton.

## Book Corner

*Buzz Said the Bee* by Wendy Cheyette Lewison

*The Giant Jam Sandwich* by John Lord

*The Honey Makers* by Gail Gibbons

✓ **Special Needs Adaptation:** Rather than using the Rebus Chart, ask the child to show you specific parts of the bee, such as the body, head, and legs. If the child does not understand how to do it, take his hand and place it on the part. Then, say the name; for example, "This is the bee's body. These are the bee's legs."

### Writing

○ Print "bee-i-ee-i-ee" on chart paper. Then print it on sheets of drawing paper, leaving blank spaces for the letter "e". Encourage the children to fill in the blanks.

# Home Connection

○ Have the children ask their families if they have honey in their kitchen. When the children return to school, use their information to make a graph to show how many children had honey in the cupboard.

# My Busy Garden

## Vocabulary

| | |
|---|---|
| ants | here |
| bee | insect |
| beetle | leaves |
| busy | pollen |
| buzz | scurry |
| chew | spider |
| chomp | spin |
| dig | there |
| flower | |
| garden | toss |

## Theme Connections

Movement
Sounds

(Tune: She'll Be Comin' 'Round the Mountain)
Oh, the ants are busy digging all around—dig, dig.
Oh, the ants are busy digging all around—dig, dig.
See them scurry here and there—tossing dirt into the air.
Oh, the ants are busy digging all around—dig, dig.

Oh, the bees are busy buzzing all around—buzz, buzz.
Oh, the bees are busy buzzing all around—buzz, buzz.
See them buzzing here and there—lots of pollen in the air.
Oh, the bees are busy buzzing all around—buzz, buzz.

Oh, spiders are busy spinning all around—spin, spin.
Oh, spiders are busy spinning all around—spin, spin.
See them spinning low and high—better look out Mr. Fly.
Oh, the spiders are busy spinning all around—spin, spin.

Oh, the beetles are busy chewing all around—chomp, chomp!
Oh, the beetles are busy chewing all around—chomp, chomp!
See them chewing leaves and flowers—as they while away the hours.
Oh, the beetles are busy chewing all around—chomp, chomp!

Oh, the insects are all busy in my garden—way busy!
Oh, the insects are all busy in my garden—way busy!
Oh, my garden is a buzzin' with insects by the dozen.
Oh, the insects are all busy in my garden—way, busy!

## Did You Know?

### Ants

❍ Ants spend most of their lives forging tunnels and nesting.

### Bees

❍ Bees buzz for several reasons. Their wings make noise by flapping so they can hear each other. The buzzing serves to warn away other animals who want to steal honey. Because bees die after stinging, it is better for the bee to warn intruders before stinging; that way, the bee lives to buzz another day.

### Beetles

○ Lady beetles, ladybugs, or ladybird beetles are among the most visible and best known beneficial predatory insects. Over 450 species are found in North America. Some are native and some have been introduced from other countries.

### Spiders

○ Spider webs are made of continuous strands of spider silk produced from six silk glands beneath the abdomen. A web-spinning spider first constructs a web framework and attaches it to parts of plants or other firm supports. This framework has threads radiating out from the center. Next, the spider works from the edge of the web toward the center laying down a spiral of sticky threads.

○ See page 96 for more information about spiders. See pages 22 and 94 for more information about ants, pages 16 and 95 for more information about bees, and page 95 for more information about beetles.

# Literacy Links

### Comprehension

○ Challenge children to add a verse to the song about crickets.

○ Say a sentence about one of the insects or bugs in the song without using the insect or bug's name. Can the children guess which insect or bug you are talking about?

### Oral Language

○ Discuss the things that keep insects busy. *How do they move? What jobs do they do? What do they eat?*

○ Discuss the difference between flower beds and gardens. *Do insects live in both places? Where is a bee more likely to live? Where is the beetle more likely to live?*

### Phonological Awareness

○ Discuss the *onomatopoeic* sounds (words that sound like the sounds they are describing) in the song. Ask the children to name other insects and demonstrate the sounds that they make.

# Curriculum Connections

### Art

○ Use glue to design spider webs. Allow it to dry. Provide paper and crayons and encourage the children to rub over the designs to create their own spider webs.

### Discovery

○ Search around outside until you find a good spider web, preferably one that is no longer in use. Spray both sides of the web with enamel paint (adult only). Be careful not to spray too heavily or the web will tear under the weight of the paint. Hold a piece of paper or tagboard against the wet web. It should stick to the wet paint. Carefully cut web strands that attach the web to a structure or plant. Lay the paper down until the web is dry. **Note:** Make sure children are at a distance when you spray the enamel paint.

○ Place a few ants in a jar of wet sand and a few in a jar of dry sand. Close the lids and observe. *Do the ants work better with wet or dry sand?* (Release the ants outside as soon as possible.) Provide a tub of wet sand and a tub of dry sand and digging tools such as shovels, spoons, sticks, and scoops for the children to explore. *Which sand is easier to dig?* Discuss how an ant digs. *How does the ant move the dirt?*

### Fine Motor

○ Provide playdough and pipe cleaners. Encourage the children to make insects.

### Games

○ Make two photocopies of the Bug Pattern Cards (pages 105-106). Pick out several cards, paying specific attention to selecting those insects mentioned in the song. Color them, cut them apart, and laminate them. Invite the children to play Bug Concentration.

### Gross Motor

○ Make a large spider web by stretching white yarn between chairs and table legs. Invite the children to crawl through the web without touching the yarn. After they crawl, suggest that they scoot, walk, and then jump through the web maze.

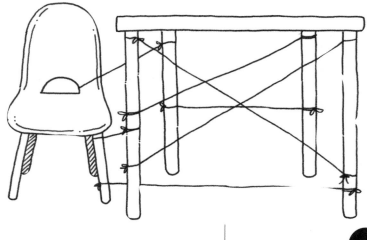

## Book Corner

### Listening

❍ Give the children items to create buzzing sounds; for example, wax paper and a comb; a kazoo; an empty toilet paper tube; and a kitchen timer. Ask them to select the buzzing sound they think sounds most like a bee.

✓ **Special Needs Adaptation:** Adapt this activity by telling the children that when you make an insect noise, they should move around—dance, rock, wave their hands, or any other movement— and when you stop making the insect noise, they are to freeze. This builds listening skills and motor skills at the same time. Remember to model the activity a couple of times so the children know what you expect of them.

### Science

❍ Provide a picture of a bee, a beetle, a spider, and an ant. Photocopy and laminate the Rebus Insect Checklist (page 118). Encourage the children to check the list to see if any are not insects. *Which bug is missing one of the following—three body parts, two antennae, six legs, and an outer skeleton?*

# Home Connection

❍ Encourage the children to ask their families to help them check their flower beds for the bugs mentioned in the song.

# Little Ants

## Vocabulary

ants
dance
goodbye
happy
hop
join
line
long
sneak
song
spin
wave

## Theme Connections

Friends and Families
Movement
Music

## Did You Know?

○ Ants go through four growing stages: egg, larva, pupa, and adult.
○ Biologists classify ants as a special group of wasps.
○ There are over 10,000 known species of ants. Each ant colony has at least one queen. The job of the queen is to lay eggs, which the worker ants care for.
○ See page 39 in "Little Ant's Hill," page 22 in "The Ants Go Marching," and page 94 for additional information about ants.

(Tune: This Old Man)
Little ants are marching by, hurrah, hurrah,
In a line that's mighty long, hurrah, hurrah.
With a hip, hop, happy, hi,
Won't you join my song?
And the little ants are marching on and on!

Little ants are hopping by, hurrah, hurrah,
In a line that's mighty long, hurrah, hurrah.
With a hip, hop, happy, hi,
Won't you join my song?
And the little ants are hopping on and on!

Little ants are dancing by, hurrah, hurrah,
In a line that's mighty long, hurrah, hurrah.
With a hip, hop, happy, hi,
Won't you join my song?
And the little ants are dancing on and on!

Little ants are spinning by, hurrah, hurrah,
In a line that's mighty long, hurrah, hurrah.
With a hip, hop, happy, hi,
Won't you join my song?
And the little ants are spinning on and on!

Little ants are sneaking by, hurrah, hurrah,
In a line that's mighty long, hurrah, hurrah.
With a hip, hop, happy, hi,
Won't you join my song?
And the little ants are sneaking on and on!

Little ants are waving bye, hurrah, hurrah,
In a line that's mighty long, hurrah, hurrah.
With a hip, hop, happy, hi,
Won't you join my song?
And the little ants are waving goodbye!
And the little ants are waving goodbye!

**Special Needs Adaptation**: For children with cognitive disabilities, teach them each action word before introducing the song. For example, say the word *hopping* and ask the child to hop. Don't forget to explain words that may be unfamiliar, such as *sneaking*. Explain that sneaking is something you do when you do not want people to see you.

# Literacy Links

### Oral Language

❍ Invite the children to demonstrate all of the movements of the ant—spinning, dancing, hopping, and so on. Sing the song, acting out the appropriate movements as they are mentioned.

❍ Teach the children the American Sign Language sign for *ant* (page 121).

❍ Print *ant* in the middle of a sheet of chart paper. Draw a circle around the word. Ask the children to tell you what they know about ants. Write the information they share on lines that extend out from the circle.

### Phonological Awareness

❍ Print the tongue twister, "anxious ants' antics" on chart paper. Underline the first letter of each word. Point out that the repetition of a beginning consonant sound in a serious of words is called *alliteration*. Have the children say the tongue twister three times quickly. *Does it twist your tongue?*

### Print Awareness

❍ Print "Busy Ants" (page 93) on chart paper. Move your hand under the words as you read it to the children. Point out the top-to-bottom and left-to-right direction of the words of the song.

# Curriculum Connections

### Construction

❍ Give the children three connected crates from a paper egg carton. Provide pipe cleaners and paint, and invite the children to create ants.

### Discovery

❍ Give the children things that spin, such as tops, lids, spools, and buttons. Encourage them to spin each item.

### Dramatic Play

❍ Make a big box into a picnic basket. Make ant antennae out of pipe cleaners. Encourage the children to pretend to be ants around a picnic basket. Have play food available for them to carry away.

### Gross Motor

❍ Put a line of masking tape on the floor. Show children how to hop, and challenge them to hop the length of the line.

## Math

○ Place an 8' strip of masking tape on the floor. Have the children pretend to be ants and line up on the masking tape in a straight line. Ask them to count how many children are on the line. *How many children does it take to cover the line?*

## Music and Movement

○ Play classical music and invite the children to get into a crawling position and dance like ants. *Is dancing more difficult on your hands and knees or on your feet?*

○ Provide rhythm band instruments and challenge the children to create a beat to accompany the scurrying of ants.

## Science

○ Have the children look through magazines to find photographs of animals and insects that hop. *Do ants really hop? Which insects hop?*

○ Show the children a photo of an ant. Challenge them to use the Rebus Insect Checklist (page 118) to determine if the ant is an insect. *Does the ant have three body parts, two antennae, six legs, and an outer skeleton?*

## Story Time

○ Read Chris Van Allsburg's *Two Bad Ants*. Observe how ordinary objects look from an ant's perspective. Discuss what your homes and classroom might look like to an ant. Challenge the children to draw a picture of how they might appear to an ant.

## Writing

○ Print *ants* on drawing paper or index cards. Give the children plastic ants to place on top of the letters. If plastic ants are not available, allow the children to use raisins to simulate ants. When they have finished, let them eat the "ants" they used.

○ See pages 22-24 in "The Ants Go Marching" and pages 39-42 in "Little Ant's Hill" for additional ant activities.

*Ant Cities* by Arthur Dorros
*Are You an Ant?* by Judy Allen
*Hey, Little Ant* by Phillip M. Hoose
*The Little Red Ant and the Great Big Crumb: A Mexican Fable* by Shirley Climo

# Home Connection

○ Ask the children to share an ant fact with their families. When they return to school, ask them which fact they shared.

# Little Caterpillar

(Tune: The Itsy Bitsy Spider)
Fuzzy little caterpillar
Onto a weed he crept.
Spun himself a chrysalis
And quietly he slept.
When the morning sun came
He stretched and gave a sigh;
Flapped and dried his beautiful wings;
Now he's a butterfly.

## Vocabulary

beautiful
butterfly
caterpillar
chrysalis
flap
fuzzy
morning
quietly
sing
slept
stretch
sun
weed

## Theme Connection

Movement

## Did You Know?

### Butterflies

○ Butterflies are the second largest group of pollinators, next to bees.
○ A Monarch butterfly's chrysalis is green.
○ The largest threat to butterflies is loss of habitat.
○ Because butterflies are cold-blooded, it is necessary for them to warm up their flight muscles. They do this by basking in the sun to absorb heat.
○ When it rains, butterflies find shelter in dense undergrowth and tree cavities.

### Caterpillars

○ Caterpillars shed their skin as they grow, just like snakes.
○ Some people believe that when the black bands on the Woolybear caterpillar are wide, a cold winter is coming.
○ See page 35 for information about caterpillars.

## Literacy Links

### Comprehension

○ Teach the children "Metamorphosis." Discuss the process of metamorphosis.

### Metamorphosis

*I'm an egg* (curl up in fetal position)
*I'm an egg*
*I'm an egg, egg, egg.*
*I'm a worm* (open up and wiggle on the floor)
*I'm a wiggly and humpy worm.*
*I'm a cocoon* (curl up again and cover face)
*I'm a cocoon*
*I'm a round and silky cocoon.*
*I'm a butterfly* (stand and fly)
*I'm a butterfly*
*I'm a grand and glorious butterfly.*

## Oral Language

❍ Teach the children the American Sign Language signs for *caterpillar* and *butterfly* (page 121).

## Oral Language/Comprehension

❍ Make a KWL chart (page 120) for Caterpillars and Butterflies. Print *Caterpillars* and *Butterflies* at the top of a sheet of chart paper. Under the words, make a chart with three columns. Label the first column, "What We Know." Label the second column, "What We Want to Know." Label the third column, "What We Learned." Encourage the children to help you fill in the first two columns. After studying butterflies and caterpillars, you can add information to the last column.

# Curriculum Connections

## Art

❍ Draw 8" to 10" butterflies on poster board to use as a pattern. Give the children sheets of wax paper to place on top of the butterfly patterns. Have them tear small pieces of tissue paper from multi-colored sheets and then use liquid starch to adhere the pieces of tissue paper to the wax paper inside the lines of the wings, which show through the wax paper. Have them use several layers of torn paper to make the wings sturdy. When the wings are completely filled in, have the children cut a body from black construction paper and glue it between the wings. When the glue is dry, help the children carefully remove the wax paper. Hang the butterflies in a window and enjoy the lovely colors as the sun shines through them.

SONGS AND ACTIVITIES

## Construction

❍ Invite the children to make a small butterfly and its chrysalis. Help the children fold an index card in half, drop a few drops of different colors of tempera paint inside the fold, and press the folded index card to make the wings. When the paint dries, have the children use a crayon to outline the butterfly's body. Punch a small hole in the butterfly's head and thread with small segments of a pipe cleaner to create antennae. Have children paint a toilet paper tube to look like a chrysalis. Help them glue the butterfly to one end of a tongue depressor and let dry. Curl the butterfly's wings and slide it into the chrysalis. Pull the stick, and make the beautiful butterfly come out of its chrysalis! Fly the butterfly like a real one!

## Discovery

❍ Invite children to use eyedroppers to drop water colored with food coloring onto coffee filters to create designs. Call attention to how the colors spread through the filters. Remind the children that this is called *absorption*. When the filters are dry, show the children how to thread them into the slots of clothespins to make butterflies. Give the children markers to use to add eyes and pipe cleaners to use for antennae.

## Dramatic Play

❍ Provide old sleeping bags and encourage the children to pretend that the sleeping bags are cocoons.

## Games

❍ Have a cocoon-wrapping contest. Ask the children to select a partner. Give each team a roll of toilet paper. Ask them to decide who is going to be the caterpillar and who is going to be the wrapper. Say "Go!" and see who can wrap up the caterpillar first.

✓ **Special Needs Adaptation:** For some children, this game might be frightening. To demonstrate how it is done, you should be the first cocoon and let the children wrap you. This would be a good collaboration activity, once children realize it is fun and that it will not hurt them.

## Language

❍ Photocopy the Metamorphosis Sequence Cards (page 115). Color them, cut them out, and laminate them. Encourage the children to use the cards to discuss the process of metamorphosis.

## Book Corner

*Bubba and Trixie* by Lisa Campbell Ernst
*Clara Caterpillar* by Pamela Duncan Edwards
*From Caterpillar to Butterfly* by Deborah Heiligman
*Monarch Butterfly* by Gail Gibbons
*Waiting for Wings* by Lois Ehlert
*Where Butterflies Grow* by Joanne Ryder

## Math

○ Have children trace large circles on green paper. (The inside of a roll of masking tape is an easily traceable shape.) Help them number the circles from 1 to 5 and then place their circles in numerical order. The children can paste the circles together, if desired. Invite them to draw a face on the first circle and then add antennae. Let them add small strips of paper for feet.

## Music and Movement

○ Provide colorful streamers to use as butterfly wings. Play classical music and invite the children to fly like butterflies.

## Science

○ Provide a photograph of a caterpillar and a photograph of butterfly. Challenge the children to use the Rebus Insect Checklist (page 118) to determine if the caterpillar and the butterfly are insects. *Does the caterpillar have three body parts, two antennae, six legs, and an outer skeleton? Does the butterfly have three body parts, two antennae, six legs, and an outer skeleton?*

**Special Needs Adaptation:** Using the Rebus Chart may be too difficult for some children. Instead, see if they can help you sequence the life cycle of a butterfly, starting with the caterpillar stage. After you sequence the cards, see if the child can do it alone or with a peer buddy.

○ See pages 35-38 in "Fuzzy Caterpillar" for additional activities for caterpillars and butterflies.

# Home Connection

○ Make a copy of the Metamorphosis Sequence Cards (page 115) for each child. Have the children color them and help them cut the cards out. Encourage them to take the cards home to use as a prompt when talking to their families about metamorphosis.

# All Around My Yard

(Tune: The Wheels on the Bus)
The firefly at night goes blink, blink, blink,
Blink, blink, blink; blink, blink, blink.
The firefly at night goes blink, blink, blink
All around my yard.

Additional verses:
The bees in the flowers go buzz, buzz, buzz…
The ants in the grass go march, march, march…
The crickets in the leaves go chirp, chirp, chirp…
The caterpillar in the field goes creep, creep, creep…
The worm in the dirt goes munch, munch, munch…

## Vocabulary

ants
bee
blink
buzz
caterpillar
chirp
creep
cricket
dirt
field
firefly
flower
grass
leaves
march
munch
night
worm
yard

## Theme Connections

Movement
Nighttime
Sounds

## Did You Know?

### Crickets

❍ The cricket belongs to the same family of insects as the grasshopper and katydid.

❍ While crickets have wings, the majority of them do not fly. Their wings are often too small to be of any use. Most crickets move around by jumping from place to place. Through time, they have developed legs that are built for jumping great heights in comparison to their size. Crickets vary in size, with most being in the range of ½" to 1".

### Fireflies

❍ Other common names for fireflies are *lightning bugs* and *glowworms*.

❍ It is rare to find flashing fireflies in the western United States. Although some isolated sightings have been reported, fireflies that glow are typically not found west of Kansas.

### Ants, Bees, Butterflies, and Worms

❍ See pages 16 and 51 for information about bees and pages 35 and 95 for information about butterflies. See page 97 for information about worms and page 94 for information about ants.

# Literacy Links

### Comprehension
○ Print *firefly* on chart paper. Draw a line between the words *fire* and *fly*. Point out that the word *firefly* is made up of two words, each of which can stand alone. Explain that when a word is made up of two independent words it is called a *compound word. What other insects have names that are compound words?* (butterfly, ladybug, and grasshopper)

### Oral Language
○ Encourage the children to write another verse to the song, such as "the grasshoppers hop" or "the crickets sing."
○ Teach children the American Sign Language signs for *bee, ant, caterpillar,* and *worm* (page 121).

### Oral Language/Comprehension
○ Challenge the children to write a story about a firefly that uses its light to rescue a lost child.

> ✓ **Special Needs Adaptation:** For children with cognitive disabilities, modify this activity by making pictures to accompany the main points of the story the children create. Make the sentences short. Read the story to the children with special needs. See if they can retell the story, using picture cues that you provide. Ask the child to place the picture cue cards in the correct order. Talk about what happens first, next, and so on. Talk about the beginning of the story and the end of the story.

### Phonological Awareness
○ Discuss the *onomatopoeic* sounds (words that sound like the sound they are describing) in the song. Challenge the children to think of an insect that is not mentioned in the song and create a verse to the song about that insect.

# Curriculum Connections

### Art
○ Provide markers to draw the various insects mentioned in the song. Provide fluorescent markers for the children to use to make the tail of the firefly.

○ Encourage the children to illustrate their favorite verse from the song.

### Discovery

○ Provide magazines and encourage the children to cut out pictures of insects and then sort them by how they move.

### Games

○ Play Find the Firefly. Designate one child to be the "firefly" and give her a flashlight. Turn off the lights and have everyone close their eyes while the firefly finds a place to hide. Have the children flash the flashlight off and on rapidly and encourage the rest of the children to find the firefly.

### Gross Motor

○ Invite the children to try Cricket Jumps. Make a maze of medium-sized boxes. Invite the children ("crickets") to jump through the maze while in a squatting position.

### Outdoors

○ Take a walk outside in search of insects. Make a list of the insects you find.

### Science

○ Photocopy the Rebus Insect Checklist (page 118). Color it and laminate it. Provide photos of the insects and bugs mentioned in the song and encourage the children to determine which are insects.

### Writing

○ Print *fire* and *fly* on index cards. Invite the children to put the words together to make *firefly*. Provide paper and magnetic letters. Encourage the children to trace the letters to make *firefly*.

*Bugs! Bugs! Bugs!* by Bob Barner

*Chirping Crickets* by Melvin Berger

*Fireflies* by Julie Brinckloe

*The Very Lonely Firefly* by Eric Carle

# Home Connection

○ Encourage the children to ask their families to search their yards for insects. Have them ask their families to make a list of the insects they find. Compare the lists the children bring back to school. Are there any insects that are on every child's list? Are their any bugs that are not on anyone's list?

# Can You Move With Me?

(Tune: Do Your Ears Hang Low?)
Can you wiggle like a worm?
Can you squiggle? Can you squirm?
Can you flutter? Can you fly like a gentle butterfly?
Can you crawl upon the ground
Like a beetle that is round?
Can you move with me?

Can you flip? Can you flop?
Can you give a little hop?
Can you slither like a snake?
Can you give a little shake?
Can you dance like bee
Who is buzzing round a tree?
Can you move with me?

## Vocabulary

bee
beetle
butterfly
buzz
crawl
dance
flip
flop
flutter
gentle
ground
hop
round
shake
slither
snake
squiggle
squirm
tree
wiggle
worm

## Did You Know?

○ Bees wiggle their abdomens and fly in circles around a pollen area in order to communicate the location of food to their fellow bees.

○ Ants communicate by touching each other with their antennae.

○ Grasshoppers produce acoustical signals by rubbing their hind legs against the sides of their abdomen. They may also communicate by rapidly flexing or snapping their hind wings in flight.

○ See page 96 for additional information about grasshoppers. See page 97 for additional information about worms. See pages 16, 51, and 94 for information about bees.

## Theme Connections

Movement
Sounds

# Literacy Links

### Oral Language

○ Encourage the children to demonstrate the way a variety of insects move. *Do bees and butterflies move their wings the same way? Do spiders and ants look the same when they crawl?*

○ Teach the children the American Sign Language signs for *worm*, *bee*, *snake*, and *butterfly* (page 121).

### Phonological Awareness

○ Discuss the rhyming word pairs in the song, for example, *worm/squirm*, *ground/round*, *flop/hop*, and *shake/snake*.

✓ **Special Needs Adaptation:** Learning to recognize rhyming words is very important for children with speech and language delays. To increase phonological awareness, start by making a list of simple words that rhyme, such as cup/pup, hat/cat, and can/fan. Then discuss the rhyming word pairs in the song; for example, worm/squirm, ground/round, flop/hop, and shake/snake. Look for opportunities throughout the daily routine to point out rhyming words. For example, make up words that rhyme with the names of the children in the class, such as Matt/cat, Sue/shoe, and Tamika/Topeka.

### Segmentation

○ Jump to the syllables in "wiggle worm," "buzzing bees," and "shaky snake."

# Curriculum Connections

### Construction

○ Help the children make worms. Cut toilet paper tubes in half and invite the children to decorate each section. Help the children string five sections together by punching two holes in the end of the sections and then tying them together with yarn. Invite the children to wiggle their worms.

### Fine Motor

○ Encourage the children to draw designs on two sheets of drawing paper. Show them how to fold their drawings into fans. Invite them to use the fans to flutter like butterflies.

### Games

○ Make a copy of the Insect Pattern Cards (pages 105-106). Enlarge the individual cards. Color the insects and laminate the cards. Use the card to play a modified game of Charades. Hold up a card and invite a volunteer to move like the insect or bug you are holding. Ask a second volunteer to tell you a fact about the insect or bug.

> **English Language Learner Strategy:** Hold up one of the insect cards. Say the name of the insect and encourage the child to repeat the name of the insect.

### Gross Motor

○ Stuff six knee-high stockings with crumpled paper to make worms. Tie off the end of each stocking. Cut a large leaf from bulletin board paper and place it in the middle of the floor. Make a throw line on the floor with masking tape. Ask the children to toss the worms one at a time, trying to make each worm land on the leaf. After each child has a turn, count the worms that landed on the leaf and those that landed off the leaf. *Did more leaves land on the leaf or off the leaf?*

○ Drape a sheet over a table to make a tunnel. Have the children crawl through the tunnel like a beetle.

○ Worms move by lengthening the front part of their body, then pulling up the back part. Challenge the children to move like a worm.

### Language

○ Use the bee pattern on page 105 to make five paper bees. Make a Bee Glove by taping each bee to one of the fingers of a work glove. Teach the children the fingerplay, "The Beehive" (page 93). Give the Bee Glove to the children and let them re-enact the fingerplay.

> **English Language Learner Strategy:** Make paper bees and tape them to your fingers. Show the children how the bees can be hidden to familiarize children with the new vocabulary. Show a picture of a beehive and demonstrate how your hand is clasped to look like a hive. Recite the rhyme and model the actions with your fingers. Invite the children to join in the fingerplay as you say it a second time. If children begin to use the words, note the language they use.

### Science

○ Provide photos of worms, bees, beetles, snakes, and butterflies. Photocopy the Rebus Insect Checklist (page 118), color, and laminate it. Have the children use the checklist to determine if the bugs mentioned in the song are insects or bugs.

### Writing

○ Print *worm* on drawing paper. Provide playdough. Encourage the children to roll worms to place over the letters in the word. Cover the letters with worms.

○ See pages 52, 53, and 17 for additional activities about bees. See page 32 for additional activities about worms. See pages 36 and 64 for additional activities about butterflies.

# Home Connection

○ Suggest that children show their families how to flutter like a butterfly and wiggle like a worm.

## Book Corner

*Diary of a Worm* by Doreen Cronin

*Ultimate Bug Book* by Luise Woelflein

*Where Butterflies Grow* by Joanne Ryder

*Wonderful Worms* by Linda Glaser

# Over in the Meadow

Over in the meadow in the sand and the sun
Lived an old mother toadie and her little toadie one.
"Wink!" said the mother. "I wink!" said the one,
So they winked and they blinked in the sand and the sun.

Over in the meadow where the stream runs blue
Lived an old father fish and his little fishes two.
"Swim!" said the father. "We swim!" said the two,
So they swam and they leaped where the stream runs blue.

Over in the meadow in a hole in a tree
Lived an old mother bluebird and her little birdies three.
"Sing!" said the mother. "We sing!" said the three,
So they sang and were glad in a hole in a tree.

Over in the meadow in the reeds on the shore
Lived an old father muskrat and his little ratties four.
"Dive!" said the father. "We dive!" said the four,
So they dived and they burrowed in the reeds on the shore.

Over in the meadow in a snug beehive
Lived a mother honey bee and her little bees five.
"Buzz!" said the mother. "We buzz!" said the five,
So they buzzed and they hummed in the snug beehive.

Over in the meadow in a nest built of sticks
Lived a black father crow and his little crows six.
"Caw!" said the father. "We caw!" said the six,
So they cawed and they called in their nest built of sticks.

Over in the meadow where the grass is so even
Lived a green mother cricket and her little crickets seven.
"Chirp!" said the mother. "We chirp!" said the seven,
So they chirped cheery notes in the grass soft and even.

Over in the meadow by the old mossy gate
Lived a brown father lizard and his little lizards eight.
"Bask!" said the father. "We bask!" said the eight,
So they basked in the sun on the old mossy gate.

*(continued on the next page)*

## Vocabulary

bask
beehive
blink
burrow
caw
cheery
chirp
cricket
den
frog
gate
glad
hum
lacy
lizard
meadow
mossy
muskrat
ratties
shine
sly
snug
spider
stream
toadie
web
wink

## Theme Connections

Animals
Counting
Habitats

BUGS, BUGS, BUGS

(continued from previous page)

Over in the meadow where the quiet pools shine
Lived a green mother frog and her little froggies nine.
"Croak!" said the mother. "We croak!" said the nine,
So they croaked and they splashed where the quiet pools shine.

Over in the meadow in a sly little den
Lived a gray father spider and his little spiders ten.
"Spin!" said the father. "We spin!" said the ten,
So they spun lacy webs in their sly little den.

# Did You Know?

○ Toads have stubby bodies with short hind legs for walking instead of hopping, warts, and dry skin (they usually prefer dryer climates).

○ Fish live and breathe in water. All fish are vertebrates (have a backbone) and most breathe through gills and have fins and scales.

○ Bluebirds are 6 ½ to 7 inches in length, and they are fatter than a sparrow. Their head, throat, wings, and tail are bright blue. Their chest and part of their back is rust red.

○ The muskrat is a large aquatic rodent native to North America. Their body is covered in thick, brown waterproof fur. They live in wetlands, such as ponds, lakes, marshes, and river banks, hence the nickname "swamp bunny."

○ See page 95 for information about bees.

○ Crows are among the most adaptable and intelligent birds in the world. They have a varied and evolved language. They can mimic the sounds made by other animals, and they learn to associate noises with events, especially with the distribution of food.

○ See page 96 for information about crickets.

○ Lizards are cold-blooded; they love to bask in the sun.

○ Frogs lay eggs that hatch into tadpoles. Seven to 10 days after the tadpole has hatched, it will begin to swim around and feed on algae. Crickets are the main diet of the adult frog but they will also eat June bugs, moths, grasshoppers, and pill bugs. Larger frog species will eat pinkies and feeder fish.

○ See pages 89 and 96 for information about spiders.

# Literacy Links

## Oral Language

○ Teach the American Sign Language signs for *frog*, *bird*, *bee*, and *spider* (page 121).

### Oral Language/Print Awareness

○ Make a list of each animal mentioned in the song. Discuss the actions of each animal.

### Phonological Awareness

○ Discuss the rhyming words in the song; for example, *one/sun*, *blue/two*, *tree/three*, *shore/four*, and so on. Select a pair of words like *blue* and *two* and have the children think of additional words that rhyme with these words.

○ Ask children to identify the *onomatopoeic* words (words that sound like the sound they are describing) in the song, for example, *croak*, *chirp*, *caw*, and *buzz*.

### Segmentation

○ Clap to the syllables in each animal name. Make a list of one-syllable and two-syllable names. *Are there more one-syllable names or two-syllable names?*

# Curriculum Connections

### Art

○ Provide crayons and encourage the children to draw their favorite animal in the song.

### Dramatic Play

○ Provide a mirror. Invite the children to explore winking. *Can you wink like a toad? How is winking different from blinking?*

○ Provide Blue Bird Puppets. Cut blue birds from blue construction paper. Use a marker to draw the beak and other features. Use small wiggle eyes for the eye. Glue the bird to a tongue depressor to create a Blue Bird Puppet. Invite the children to put on a puppet show with singing birds.

### Fine Motor

○ Provide small sticks and encourage the children to build a nest for a crow.

### Fine Motor/Math

○ Away from the children, spray paint the cup of a meatball press green. Glue wiggle eyes on the top of one of the cups. Place pompoms representing bugs in a bowl. Provide five paper plates with the numerals 1–5 written on the plates. Encourage the children to use the Toad Gobblers to pick up the right number of bugs from the bowl and move them to the appropriate plates.

### Gross Motor

○ Place a strip of masking tape on the floor as a start line. Have the children jump like crickets from the line. Place a beanbag on the floor to measure their jumps. *Which little cricket jumps the farthest?*

### Language

○ Photocopy the Over in the Meadow Patterns (pages 107-109). Color them, cut them out, and laminate them. Encourage the children to use the cards to sing the story the song tells.

### Math

○ Photocopy the Over in the Meadow Patterns (pages 107-109). Have the children match magnetic numerals to indicate the number of animals in each picture card.

### Music and Movement

○ Play Musical Lily Pads as you would play Cooperative Musical Chairs. Cut six large (3' by 6') lily pads out of green vinyl or green bulletin board paper. Tell the children that you are going to play music and when the music stops they must get on a lily pad. It is okay for more than one child to be on a lily pad. Play the music and stop. Remove a lily pad and play again. Continue until there is only one lily pad left. You may want to divide the group in half and use three lily pads for each group. After the game, lay the lily pads in a pathway and invite the children to jump like frogs from one lily pad to the next.

### Science

○ Provide photographs of a frog, bee, crow, cricket, and lizard. Photocopy the Rebus Insect Checklist (page 118) and color and laminate it. Have the children use the checklist to determine if any of the animals in the photos are insects. *Do they have the three body parts, two antennae, six legs, and an outer skeleton?*

○ See pages 48 and 90 for additional activities for spiders, pages 17 and 52 for additional activities for bees, and page 68 for additional activities for crickets.

# Home Connection

○ Encourage the children to look around their homes for animals mentioned in the song.

## Book Corner

*Frog and Toad* by Arnold Lobel

*A Frog in the Bog* by Karma Wilson

*Over in the Meadow* by Annie Kubler

*Over in the Meadow* by Ezra Jack Keats

*Over in the Meadow* by Olive A. Wadsworth

# Shoo Fly

Shoo fly, don't bother me,
Shoo fly, don't bother me,
Shoo fly, don't bother me,
Because I am a somebody!

I feel, I feel, I feel like a morning star.
I feel, I feel, I feel like a morning star.

Shoo fly, don't bother me,
Shoo fly, don't bother me,
Shoo fly, don't bother me,
Because I am a somebody!

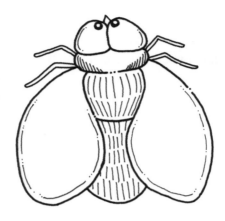

## Vocabulary

belong
bother
fly
morning star
shoo

## Theme Connections

Food and Nutrition
Friends and Families

## Did You Know?

○ The housefly is one of the most common insects. It is found worldwide and is a pest in homes, barns, dairies, poultry houses, food processing plants, and recreation areas. It has a tremendous breeding potential, and during the warmer months can produce a generation in less than two weeks.

○ The just-hatched housefly crawls about rapidly while its wings unfold and its body dries and hardens. Mating occurs immediately. A housefly may go through an entire life cycle from egg, to larva, to pupa, to winged adult in six to ten days. An adult housefly may live an average of 30 days.

○ Insects have compound eyes. Instead of one lens, they see through two spheres with many lenses. Apart from that, they often have an extra single lens eye on the front of the head. Each lens of the compound eye catches a facet of an image. The final image an insect sees is like a mosaic. The more lenses the compound eye bears, the higher the resolution of the image. A fly's two large spherical eyes give it close to 360 degree vision.

○ See page 82 for additional information about flies.

# Literacy Links

### Oral Language

○ Talk about flies. *Where do we see flies? How do we make them go away?*

○ Discuss the cliché, "I wish I could be a fly on the wall." *What does it mean?* Mention other clichés, such as "quiet as a mouse" or "chip off the old block." A cliché is an overused metaphor used and understood by lots of people. It conveys an image that is universally understood within a specific population.

○ Discuss the word *bother*. Have the children use the word in a sentence.

(✓) **Special Needs Adaptation:** In addition to discussing bother, look for other words in the song that children may not know, such as shoo. Explain the difference between the word shoo in the song and shoe that you wear on your feet. This may be especially difficult for children with Asperger's syndrome, a form of autism, who are very literal in their interpretation of language. Understanding the difference may be quite confusing. The phrase morning star may need further discussion, as well. Many children associate stars with nighttime and sun with daylight. Talk about what the phrase means; for example, a planet, such as Venus, that rises in the east in the early morning. If possible, encourage the child's family to point out the morning star.

### Phonological Awareness

○ Challenge the children to help you make a list of all the words that rhyme with *fly*.

### Print Awareness

○ Print the words to the song on chart paper. Move your hands under the words as you sing. Point out the left-to-right and top-to-bottom progression of the print.

# Curriculum Connections

### Art

○ Lay a 6' sheet of bulletin board paper outdoors on a flat, firm surface. Provide a shallow tub or pan of paint and flyswatters. Encourage the children to dip a clean flyswatter in the paint and then slap it on the bulletin board paper. What a great piece of modern art!

## Construction

○ Provide wax paper and black crayons. Cut wax paper into wing shapes. Give each child two wings and encourage them to use the black crayons to draw veins on the wings. Put the two wings together and use a warm iron to press them into one wing (adult only).

○ Challenge the children to construct their own model of a compound eye. Provide wheat paste (page 97), newspaper, paper egg cartons, aluminum foil, and paint. Turn a medium-size plastic mixing bowl upside down. Show the children how to cover the bowl with strips of newspaper and wheat paste to make a foundation. Have the children cut apart the individual crates of the egg carton and then glue them side by side to the foundation, covering the entire area. Paint the crates with brown or dark red tempera paint. Cut the foil into penny-size circles and glue them to the bottom of the egg carton crates. Now you have a model of a compound eye much like a fly's!

## Discovery

○ Provide a prism. Encourage children to look through the prism to see the world as it looks through the eyes of a fly.

## Fine Motor

○ Make two or three copies of the fly from the Bug Pattern Cards (pages 105-106). Color them, cut them out, laminate them, and cut into puzzle pieces. Use a marker to make different colored dots on the back of the pieces to each puzzle to keep the puzzle pieces from getting mixed up. Invite the children to work the puzzles.

## Book Corner

### Language
○ Photocopy the Fly Rhyming Word Game (page 110). Encourage the children to find the items that rhyme with *fly*.

### Science
○ Show the children a photograph of a fly. Photocopy the Rebus Insect Checklist (page 118), color it, and laminate it. Have the children use the checklist to determine if the fly is an insect or a bug.

### Writing
○ Print *shoo* on chart paper. Encourage the children to copy the word using magnetic letters.

# Home Connection

○ Suggest that children talk with their families about how they keep flies out of the house. *Do they have a flyswatter? Do they make sure to keep windows and doors closed? Do they clean up food as soon as people are finished eating? Do they use insect spray?* Discuss what the children found out when they return to school.

SONGS AND ACTIVITIES

# Flea Fly Flow

Flea *(Flea)*
Flea fly *(Flea fly)*
Flea fly flow *(Flea fly flow)*
Flea fly flow mosquito *(Flea fly flow mosquito)*
Oh no—no no more mosquitoes *(Oh no—no no more mosquitoes)*
Itchy itchy scratchy scratchy, ooh I got one down my backy!
*(Itchy itchy scratchy scratchy, ooh I got one down my backy!)*

Kumalata kumalata kumala mosquito
*(Kumalata kumalata kumala mosquito)*
A Beep billy otten dotten oh bo ba beaten dotten wye doan choo oo
*(A Beep billy otten dotten oh bo ba beaten dotten wye doan choo oo)*

Shhhhh! *(Shhhhh!)*
Chase that *(Chase that)*
Big bad bug *(Big bad bug)*
Make it go away! *(Make it go away!)*
SHOO! SHOO!
SHOO! SHOO!

## Vocabulary

back
flea
flow
fly
itchy
mosquito
scratchy

## Theme Connections

Sounds
Spatial Relationships

## Did You Know?

○ Mosquito is Spanish for "little fly." There are 3,000 kinds of mosquitoes and a worldwide population of 100 trillion mosquitoes!

○ Most mosquitoes live in tropical climates, but there are mosquitoes in the Arctic and in the desert.

○ Mosquitoes can fly up to 10 miles per hour. They can dart between raindrops and fly backwards.

○ Most mosquitoes live and die close to where they hatch, but they are capable of flying a great distance in search of food. In their quest for blood, mosquitoes may bite birds, frogs, snakes, and mammals, including people.

○ See pages 19 and 28 for more information about mosquitoes and page 78 for more information about flies.

# Literacy Links

## Comprehension/Print Awareness

O Encourage children to think of words that describe mosquitoes. Make a list of their words. Challenge the children to use "mosquito" in a sentence.

> ✓ **Special Needs Adaptation:** For children with cognitive challenges or language delays, make a list of five sentences that describe mosquitoes. Read each sentence to the child. Ask him to repeat the sentence. Then, make up a fill-in-the-blank sentence. For example, after reading the sentence, "A mosquito bites people," ask the child to fill in the blank, "A mosquito _____ people."

## Oral Language

O Teach the children the American Sign Language signs for *mosquito* (page 122).

## Phonological Awareness

O Say "flea fly flow," emphasizing the beginning sound of each word. Ask the children what sound they hear. Point out that the repetition of letter sounds at the beginning of several words in a row is called *alliteration*. At another time, teach the children the same lesson using "kumalata kumalata kumala." Teach the children a tongue twister like "Peter Piper" or "She Sells Seashells."

# Curriculum Connections

## Discovery

O Provide several items that might be used as back scratchers, such as a cardboard coat hanger tube, a back brush, a straw, or an actual back scratcher Invite the children to select the scratcher they like best.

## Dramatic Play/Water and Sand

O Provide spray bottles, bottles of scented water, spoons, funnels, and other equipment. Encourage the children to pretend they are scientists who are researching and developing a new mosquito repellent.

## Book Corner

### Games

○ Make two photocopies of the Bug Pattern Cards (pages 105-106). Color them, cut them out, and laminate them. Give the cards to the children and encourage them to play Bug Concentration.

### Language

○ Photocopy and enlarge the mosquito and fly in the Bug Pattern Cards (page 105). Color them, cut them out, laminate them and cut them into puzzle pieces. Use different colored markers to mark the pieces that go with each puzzle so the pieces do not get mixed up. When the children have completed the puzzle, ask them to name the bug. Have them identify the insect parts.

### Science

○ Use the Mosquito Life Span Sequence Cards (pages 112-114) to discuss the life cycle of the mosquito. First, the female mosquito drops her eggs into water. A *wriggler* hatches from each egg. It eats tiny animals in the water. In a week, the *wriggler* changes into a *pupa,* which floats just under the water. In a few days, the *pupa's* skin splits down the back, and a *winged adult mosquito* emerges. Challenge the children to sequence the cards.

### Snack

○ Provide large eyedroppers, juice, and empty cups. Encourage the children to fill their juice cup using an eyedropper as a mosquito mouthpiece. How long does it take?

### Writing

○ Place a tray of wet sand on the table. Print *mosquito* on index cards. Provide craft sticks and encourage the children to use the sticks as writing tools to write *mosquito* in the sand.

# Home Connection

○ Encourage children to teach their families the sign for *mosquito* (page 122).

# Five Little Ladybugs

## Vocabulary

| | |
|---|---|
| admire | ladybugs |
| alone | one |
| bathe | sea |
| dance | shore |
| dip | telephone |
| five | three |
| four | two |
| jive | view |

## Theme Connections

Counting
Friends and Families
Oceans

(Tune: Five Little Ducks)
Five little ladybugs dancing on the shore,
One danced away and then there were four.
Four little ladybugs dipping in the sea
One chased a fish and then there were three.
Three little ladybugs admiring the view
One skipped off and then there were two,
Two little ladybugs bathing in the sun
One flew home, leaving only one.
One little ladybug all alone.
She called her friends on the telephone.
They came back, now there's five
　　　To dance and sing the ladybug jive!

**Special Needs Adaptation:** For children with cognitive delays, use this song as an opportunity to reinforce numeracy skills. The song talks about five ladybugs. Use the ladybug pattern (page 105) to cut out five ladybugs. Invite the children to count them. Then ask them to hand you three ladybugs or two ladybugs. Look for other things around the room that the children can count. The more they practice counting objects, the sooner they will learn one-to-one correspondence.

## Did You Know?

- There are some 5,000 different kinds of ladybugs worldwide, 400 of which live in North America.
- The ladybug is the official state insect of Delaware, Massachusetts, New Hampshire, Ohio, and Tennessee.
- Ladybugs are members of the beetle family. They are helpful to farmers and gardeners and are not considered pests.
- A female ladybug will lay more than 1000 eggs in her lifetime. The male ladybug is usually smaller than the female.
- A ladybug beats its wings 85 times a second when it flies. Ladybugs will not fly if the temperature is below 55 degrees.
- Ladybugs chew from side to side and not up and down like people chew. Aphids are a ladybug's favorite food.
- Ladybugs make a chemical that smells and tastes terrible so birds and other predators will not eat them.
- The spots on a ladybug fade with age.

# Literacy Links

### Comprehension

❍ Print *ladybug* on chart paper. Draw a line between *lady* and *bug*. Point out that each word is a word by itself. Explain that when two words that could stand alone are put together they are called *compound words*. Provide other examples of compound words such as *doghouse*, *doorbell*, and *pigtail*. Challenge the children to think of other words that might be compound words.

### Oral Language

❍ Talk about the belief that ladybugs are good luck. Some people believe if a ladybug lands on you, you can make a wish and it will come true. Ask the children what they would wish for if a ladybug landed on them.

❍ Teach children the American Sign Language sign for *ladybug* (page 122).

### Print Awareness

❍ Print the following "Ladybug, Ladybug" rhyme on chart paper and read it to the children. Move your hand under the words as you read. Call attention to the left-to-right and top-to-bottom movement of the words.

> *Ladybug, Ladybug*
> *Ladybug, ladybug, fly away home!*
> *Your house is on fire and your children are alone.*

**Note:** Talk with the children about what they should do if they see a fire (call 911).

# Curriculum Connections

### Art

❍ Have the children draw a picture of something they would wish for if a ladybug landed on their shoulder. Encourage them to dictate their wish and, with their permission, transcribe their descriptions on the back of their pictures.

## Construction/Games

○ Turn three 6" paper bowls upside down. Ask the children to paint each paper bowl with red tempera paint. Provide glue, black markers, and construction paper for the children to use to add spots, a head, and legs. Show the children how to play Ladybug Lucky Guess. Place three ladybugs (bowls) on the table. Hide a penny under one ladybug. Move the ladybugs all around, and then invite a volunteer to guess which ladybug is hiding the penny.

## Games

○ Play Ladybug, Ladybug, Fly Away Home as you would play Musical Chairs. Have the children sit in a circle on carpet squares. Tell them that when you say, "Ladybug, ladybug, fly away home," they should stand up and fly away from the circle. While they are moving, remove one of the carpet squares. Then say, "Ladybug, ladybug, come back home." The children should return to the circle and sit on a carpet square. Children may share a carpet square with a friend. Play the game until there are two children on each carpet square.

## Language

○ Make one enlarged photocopy of the ladybug pattern from the Bug Pattern Cards (pages 105-106) for each child to color. Have them cut out their bugs and glue them to a tongue depressor to make a stick puppet. Invite the children to make their ladybugs dance.

## Science

○ Provide a picture of a ladybug. Challenge children to use the Rebus Insect Checklist (page 118) to determine if the ladybug is an insect. *Does the ladybug have three body parts, two antennae, six legs, and an outer skeleton?*

## Snack

○ Invite the children to make Ladybug Cookies. Provide red icing, wafer cookies, and candy dot decorations. Have the children ice the wafer cookie and then place the dots on the cookie to make it look like a ladybug. Eat the yummy ladybugs!

## Book Corner

○ Help the children make Ladybug Apples. Give each child half of an apple, a cherry, and four raisins. Have the children turn their apple skin side up and place the cherry at one end of the apple to form the ladybug's head. Provide whipped cream for the children to dab on in four areas to create the ladybug spots. Have them place the raisins on top of the dabs of whipped cream.

### Writing

○ Print *lady* and *bug* on index cards. Invite the children to put the cards together to form *ladybug*. Provide red finger paint and encourage the children to cover the letters in ladybug with fingerprints.

# Home Connection

○ Have children ask their family members if they have ever made a wish on a ladybug. If the answer is yes, ask them to inquire about the wish.

# Itsy Bitsy Spider

## Vocabulary

down
gigantic
itsy bitsy
rain
spider
sun
up
wash out
waterspout

## Theme Connections

Opposites
Spatial Relationships
Weather

The itsy bitsy spider
Climbed up the waterspout.
Down came the rain
And washed the spider out.
Out came the sun
And dried up all the rain.
And the itsy bitsy spider
Climbed up the spout again!

The itsy bitsy spider
Climbed to the very top,
Hesitated for a moment
But she never stopped.
When she reached her goal
She waved to all her friends,
Feeling proud inside she
Climbed up the wall again!

## Did You Know?

❍ Spiders are believed to have existed for more than 300 million years.
❍ Web-building spiders typically have three claws on the end of each leg. The middle claw and a small tuft of hairs help the spider cling to its web.
❍ Web-building spiders have two or more pairs of glands, called *spinnerets*, in their abdomens that produce liquid silk. Each *spinneret* has many small tubes. The spider spins a watery fluid, which becomes hard as soon as it hits the air. Two kinds of silk come out. One silk is dry and will not stretch; the other is sticky and stretches. Insects are caught and held by the sticky strand. Besides using the silk to wrap their egg sacs, the threads are used for draglines, wrapping insects, web trap doors, and as nest liners.
❍ See page 96 for more information about spiders.

## Literacy Links

### Oral Language

❍ Discuss waterspouts. *What do they look like? Is there more than one type of waterspout?*
❍ Talk about the number of legs on a spider. *How many pair of shoes would a spider need? How many pairs of skates?*
❍ Teach the children the American Sign Language sign for *spider* (page 122).

❍ Discuss the lesson that accompanies the song—persistence and determination. Encourage the children to identify something that has required them to be persistent.

✓ **Special Needs Adaptation:** This lesson is especially important for children with special needs who often find it more difficult to accomplish even the simplest of tasks. Talk about how the spider kept trying. Make a few small itsy bitsy spiders and keep them handy. Each time a child has difficulty doing something and seems about ready to give up, give him an itsy bitsy spider and remind him that the itsy bitsy spider kept trying. When the child accomplishes something, praise him verbally and remind him that he is just like the itsy bitsy spider in the song.

### Phonological Awareness
❍ After you sing about an itsy bitsy spider, sing the song again about a "teenie weenie" spider. Discuss the rhyming words "itsy bitsy" and "teenie weenie." Help the children create rhyming names for themselves.

### Print Awareness
❍ Print *itsy bitsy* on chart paper. Ask the children to identify the letters in each word that are the same. *Which letters are different?*

# Curriculum Connections

### Construction
❍ Encourage the children to make Spider Hats. Cut pieces of construction paper to make headbands. Cut 1" x 12" strips of construction paper and show the children how to fold the strips accordion-style. Have the children glue eight strips to their headband.

❍ Show the children how to make Wiggle Spiders. Twist four pipe cleaners in the middle to form eight legs. Attach a 12" piece of elastic thread. Show the children how to make their spiders dance.

### Dramatic Play
❍ Provide a light source. Show the children how to make shadow spiders by wiggling their fingers between the light source and the wall. Encourage them to re-enact the song.

### Fine Motor

○ Provide playdough and encourage the children to make a spider. Show them how to roll balls for the body and snakes for the legs.

### Gross Motor

○ Draw a large spider web on an old sheet. Take the sheet outdoors and use it like a parachute. Have the children stand in a circle around the parachute web and hold it with two hands. Lift up the web and say, "Red spiders run under," referring to children wearing red. Continue, naming the colors of the children's clothing.

### Language

○ Photocopy the Itsy Bitsy Spider Sequence Cards (pages 116-117). Color the cards, cut them apart, and laminate them. Encourage the children to use the cards to sequence the events in the song.

 **English Language Learner Strategy:** Have the children use the Itsy Bitsy Spider Sequence Cards to sing the song to you.

### Music and Movement

○ Have the children bend at the waist and touch their hands to the floor. Put on some music and invite the children to dance a Spider Dance.

### Outdoors

○ Take the children for a walk around the school and neighborhood to look for waterspouts.

### Science

○ Provide a photo of a spider. Photocopy the Rebus Insect Checklist (page 118). Have the children use the checklist to determine if the spider is an insect or a bug. *How many legs does the spider have? How many body parts?*

# Home Connection

○ Make a photocopy of the Itsy Bitsy Spider Sequence Cards (pages 116-117) and allow the children to color the cards and cut them apart. Send the cards home so children can use the cards to tell the spider's story to their family.

*Isty Bitsy Spider* by Iza Trapani
*Itsy Bitsy Spider* by Lorrianne Siomades
*Miss Spider's Tea Party* by David Kirk

SONGS AND ACTIVITIES

# More Learning and Fun

## Songs

### Baby Bumblebee, original version

I'm bringing home a baby bumblebee,
Won't my mommy be so proud of me, *(cup hands together as if holding bee)*
I'm bringing home a baby bumblebee,
Ouch! It stung me! *(shake hands as if just stung)*

I'm squishing up the baby bumblebee,
Won't my mommy be so proud of me, *("squish" bee between palms of hands)*
I'm squishing up a baby bumblebee,
Ooh! It's yucky! *(open up hands to look at "mess")*

I'm wiping off the baby bumblebee,
Won't my mommy be so proud of me, *(wipe hands on shirt)*
I'm wiping off the baby bumblebee,
Now my mommy won't be mad at me! *(hold up hands to show they are clean)*

### The Fuzzy Caterpillar

(Tune: Itsy Bitsy Spider)
The fuzzy caterpillar
Curled upon a leaf,
Spun her little chrysalis
And then fell asleep.
While she was sleeping,
She dreamed that she could fly,
And later when she woke up
She was a butterfly!

### Little Miss Muffet

Little Miss Muffet sat on a tuffet
Eating her curds and whey;
Along came a spider,
Who sat down beside her,
And frightened Miss Muffet away.

(New verse)
Little Miss Muffet went back to her tuffet,
Looked the thing square in the eye.
"See here, you big spider,
Miss Muffet's a fighter.
And you're the one saying bye-bye."

### One Elephant

Children sit in a circle. One child places one arm out in front to make a trunk, and walks around the circle while the group sings the song. When the group sings "called for another elephant to come," the first child chooses another to become an "elephant." The first child extends her free hand between her legs to make a tail. The second child extends one arm to make a trunk and grabs hold of the first child's tail. The two walk trunk-to-tail as the song continues.

One elephant went out to play,
Out on a spider's web one day.
He had such enormous fun,
He called for another elephant to come.

# Poems and Chants

## Arabella Miller

Little Arabella Miller
Had a fuzzy caterpillar.
First it crawled upon her mother.
Then upon her baby brother.
They said, "Arabella Miller!
Put away your caterpillar!"

## Busy Ants

Busy ants are everywhere.
Up the tree, and down the stair.
Hiding in the garden hose
And even biting at my toes.

## Garden Snail

Slowly, slowly, very slowly, goes the garden snail.
Slowly, slowly, very slowly, up the garden rail.

## Nature Walk

Going for a walk is so much fun.
We don't hurry and we don't run.
We look at all the pretty trees
And listen for birds and buzzing bees.

## Mosquitoes Inside

Don't try to eat mosquitoes,
They really aren't that yummy.
And if they get inside you,
They'll bite you in the tummy.

## Testy Termites

Testy termites tapping on my door.
Testy termites rapping on my floor.
You're too noisy to ignore.
Fly away! Fly away! Return no more!

# Fingerplays

## The Beehive

Here is a beehive, *(hold up fist)*
Where are the bees?
Hiding inside where nobody sees.
Watch and you'll see them come out of the hive
    *(open hand, one finger at a time)*
One…two…three…four…five!

## Buggy Count

1, 2, 3, *(hold up fingers)*
There's a bug on me! *(point to shoulder)*
Where did it go? *(brush off)*
    don't know. *(shrug shoulders and look puzzled)*

## Once I Saw An Anthill

Once I saw an anthill
With no ants about; *(shrug shoulders)*
So I said, "Dear little ants
Won't you please come out?" *(use hand to
    beckon)*

Then as if the little ants
Had heard my call, *(hand by ear)*
One, two, three, four, five came out,
And that was all. *(hold up fingers one to five)*

# Story

## Bessie Bee's Bell

Bessie is a honeybee. Her job is to gather pollen and take it back to the hive so it can be turned into honey. She is the best pollen gatherer of her family. She is the best pollen gatherer of the entire hive.

Bessie's best friend is Betty. Betty is blind but she still helps gather honey. She depends on Bessie to help her.

All the other bees know where the honey is because they can see their friends wiggle their bottoms and fly around the discovered pollen. Betty waits until she feels Bessie come beside her and nudges her in the right direction.

One day when the wind was blowing hard, Bessie had a difficult time flying to nudge her friend. The strong wind made her very tired. She thought, I need a better way to help Betty know where to fly.

She thought about it all day but could not think of a better plan. She had almost given up when she heard a bell ring. She looked and saw a little boy tossing jingle bells on his back porch. She waited until the boy went indoors and then she swooped down and picked up a bell. Now her only problem was how on earth she could attach the bell to her body!

All throughout the night, Bessie tried to think of a way to attach the bell to her body. In the morning on her way to pick up Betty, she had a glorious idea. She stopped by her spider friend Ava's web and asked her if she could spin her a thread that she could use to tie the bell to her bottom. Ava was more than happy to help.

When Bessie picked up Betty for their day of honey-gathering, Betty heard her coming. Betty loved the new means of communication. She flew right behind Bessie all day, and between the two of them they collected more pollen than all the other bees put together.

# Facts Related to Bugs, Bugs, Bugs!

## Ants

- Each colony of ants has its own scent. In this way, intruders can be recognized immediately. Many ants, such as the common red species, have a sting that they use to defend their nest.
- The common black ants and wood ants have no sting, but they can squirt formic acid. Some birds put ants in their feathers because the ants squirt formic acid, which gets rid of parasites.
- Carpenter ants are black or reddish black, have large jaws, and are among the largest ants. They prefer moist, soft wood that has begun to decay but may also attack newly built structures. Carpenter ants do not eat wood, they simply dig into it to create a nesting place. The resulting piles of sawdust produced often contain parts of ant bodies.
- The abdomen of the ant contains two stomachs. One stomach holds the ant's food, and second stomach holds food to share with other ants.
- Like all insects, the outside of an ant's body is covered with a hard armor called the exoskeleton.

○ An ant brain has about 250,000 brain cells; a human brain has 10,000 million brain cells.

## Bees

○ There are thousands of different kinds of bees. They are found everywhere in the world except the North and South Poles.
○ Bees buzz for several reasons. Their wings make noise by flapping so they can hear each other. The buzzing serves to warn away other animals who want to steal honey.

### How to Avoid Bee Stings

○ To avoid bee stings:
   ○ Wear light-colored, smooth-finish clothing.
   ○ Avoid perfumed soaps, shampoos, and deodorants. Do not wear cologne or perfume. Avoid bananas and banana-scented toiletries.
   ○ Wear clean clothing and bathe daily. Sweat angers bees.
   ○ Avoid flowering plants.
   ○ Keep areas clean. Social bees (What are social bees?) thrive in places where humans discard food. Clean up picnic tables, grills, and other outdoor eating areas.
   ○ If a single stinging insect is flying around, remain still. Slowly cover your face, which is the most likely place for a bee or wasp to sting. Swinging or swatting at an insect may cause it to sting you!
   ○ If you are attacked by several stinging insects at once, run away from them. Bees release a chemical when they sting. This alerts other bees to the intruder, and more bees often follow. If this happens, go indoors or jump into water. Outdoors, a shaded area is preferable to an open area for getting away from the insects. If a bee gets inside your vehicle, stop the car slowly and open all of the windows.
○ If you are stung by a bee, wash the sting site with soap and water. Remove the stinger by using a piece of gauze to wipe over it. The gauze should remove the stinger. If the gauze does not work, use your fingernail or a credit card to gently scrape over the area. Do not squeeze the stinger or use tweezers. This will cause more venom to go into the skin and injure the muscle. Apply ice to reduce swelling. Do not scratch the sting. This will cause the site to swell and itch more, and increase the chance of infection.

## Beetles

○ Most lady beetles (ladybugs) in North America are beneficial as both adults and larvae, feeding primarily on aphids. They also feed on mites, small insects, and insect eggs. The two exceptions are the introduced Mexican bean beetle and the squash beetle. The adults and larvae of both these species feed on plants.
○ Beetles, like all insects, have a head, thorax, and abdomen, and six legs. Their bodies tend to be solid and tough. They have chewing mouth parts and often have powerful jaws. Adult beetles have modified wings; the first pair of wings is small and very hard and acts as a protective covering for the second pair of wings.
○ Many beetles can fly with their second pair of wings. Most adult beetles are brown or black, but some are very brightly colored. Beetle larvae resemble worms, but they have six legs and a hard head. Beetle pupa cannot move and are covered with a leathery skin.

## Butterflies

○ Butterfly derives from the Old English word Buttorfleoge.
○ Monarchs have been known to migrate over 1850 miles (3,000 kilometers). In fact, a Monarch tagged in southern Ontario was recovered in Mexico and is on record for the longest insect migration. Monarchs can fly 621 miles (1,000 kilometers) without stopping. The Monarch's Mexican wintering site was only discovered in 1975. Males never return from migration.

○ The Painted Lady is the most widespread butterfly species in the world, appearing on all continents accept South America and Antarctica.

○ Butterflies cannot bite or chew. Like most moths, they have a long straw-like structure called a proboscis, which they use to drink nectar and juice. When not in use, the proboscis remains coiled like a garden hose.

## Crickets

○ Crickets, grasshoppers, and katydids all have excellent vision and hearing. Their compound eyes enable them to see in many directions at once. There are more than 10,000 species of the three, with the cricket making up approximately 1,000 of the species. The remaining 9,000 are split almost evenly among the grasshopper and katydid, with the grasshopper having a slight lead.

○ Crickets are said to foretell good luck and their songs are said to bring blessings to all who are lucky enough to hear them. In many parts of the world, a cricket found in the house is treated with respect. Some place them in small cages made especially for crickets and give them food and water. The longer they live, the more good luck they bring. Others leave them as they are, and believe that if the cricket stays, it means large amounts of money will come to the owners of the dwelling.

## Grasshoppers

○ A grasshopper can leap 20 times the length of its own body! If humans could do that, we could jump almost 40 yards!

○ Grasshoppers can grow to the size of 4⅓ inches.

○ Grasshoppers have two sets of wings. Some grasshoppers rub their wings together to create music, others snap their wings together while flying, and others just rub their hind legs across their front wings.

○ Some grasshoppers will only eat certain types of plants. Others will eat any plant they can find. Grasshoppers can destroy entire crops of alfalfa, clover, cotton, corn, and other grains, causing millions of dollars in crop damages every year.

○ A grasshopper's enemies include various kinds of flies that lay their eggs in or near grasshopper eggs. After the fly eggs hatch, the newborn flies eat the grasshopper eggs. Other enemies of grasshoppers include beetles, birds, mice, snakes, and spiders.

## Fireflies

○ Fireflies are beetles, not flies. Flies, such as houseflies, have one pair of wings, while all other winged insects have two pairs of wings, or four wings altogether.

○ Fireflies produce light through a chemical reaction consisting of Luciferin (a substrate) combined with Luciferase (an enzyme), ATP (adenosine triphosphate) and oxygen. When these components are combined, light is produced.

○ Many firefly species are found around water, such as ponds, streams, marshes, or even depressions, and ditches that may retain moisture longer then surrounding areas. Fireflies are also found in very dry regions.

## Fleas

○ The female flea consumes 15 times her own body weight in blood every day.

○ If you see one flea, there may be more than 100 offspring or adults looming nearby in furniture, corners, cracks, carpets, or on your pet.

## Spiders

○ Spiders that spin an orb-shaped web are called orb-web spiders. The wheel-shaped web is used to catch prey that flies into the sticky silk. The web vibrates, announcing a catch, and the spider rushes to tie up the victim before it gets away or tears the web.

○ The spider holds onto the silk thread with the claw-like bristles on its legs. Its body oil keeps it from sticking to the web. A moth is protected from the sticky strand by scales on its body. Most garden spiders hide during the day and recline in their webs at night.

○ A spider's thread is stronger than the same thickness of steel.

○ Baby spiders can make perfect webs shortly after hatching.

○ Spiders begin spinning their webs in the evening or early morning before flying insects are airborne.

○ There are four methods spiders use to capture prey. Sedentary spiders living in silk-lined burrows leap out to capture passing insects; some active spiders lie in ambush on plants, tree bark, on the ground, or under stones; some spiders, like hunters, go in search of their prey. Finally, many spiders spin webs to entrap their prey.

○ While only a few spiders in the United States are really dangerous to humans, there are significant numbers of dangerous spiders around the world. The black widow and recluse spiders have toxic venom that can be life-threatening to humans. Some wolf spiders in South America, and some running spiders worldwide have venom that causes painful symptoms in humans. Pigeon spiders of West Africa have very painful bites. In Australia, there are between 50 and 100 venomous species, at least two of which can be life-threatening to humans, the red-back and the Sydney funnel-spider.

○ Within Arachnida, spiders are classified into a special group called the Araneae that separates them from the ticks, mites, and scorpions. A distinguishing characteristic of spiders (Araneae) is their very slender waist, or pedicel, separating the cephalothorax from the abdomen.

## Worms

○ The size of a well-fed adult earthworm depends on the kind of worm it is, how many segments it has, how old it is, and how well fed it is. Some worms will be 3½ to 12 inches (90-300 millimeters) long. The largest earthworm recorded to date was found in South Africa and measured 22 feet from its nose to the tip of its tail.

○ Worms tunnel deeply in the soil and bring subsoil closer to the surface, mixing it with topsoil. Slime, a secretion of earthworms, contains nitrogen. Nitrogen is an important nutrient for plants. The sticky slime helps to hold clusters of soil particles together in formations called aggregates.

# Recipes

### Ants
Use cherry tomatoes for three body segments and pretzels for legs and antennae to make ants for snack.

### Fruit Caterpillars
Provide each child with a craft stick. Encourage them to thread sliced bananas, melon balls, grapes, and strawberries onto the stick. Provide toothpicks with raisins on the end of them for antennae.

### Wheat Paste
Prepare 1 cup of very hot water. Make a thin mixture of 3 tablespoons wheat flour and cold water. Pour the cold mixture slowly into the hot water while stirring constantly. Bring to a boil. When it thickens, allow to cool. Smear on like any other glue. For slightly better strength, add 1 tablespoon of sugar after the glue is thickened. After using a portion, reheat the remaining in a covered jar or container to sterilize it for storage or keep refrigerated. If wheat flour is not available, other flours will work.

# Honey Balls Rebus

(Using a rebus makes it easier for English language learners to follow directions.)

## Honey Balls

1/2 cup peanut butter

1/2 cup honey

1 cup nonfat powdered milk

Mix ingredients well.

Roll into balls and chill before eating.

Squeeze and pull until shiny and soft.

Enjoy!

# Mosquito Shakes Rebus

Mosquito Shakes

1 cup of strawberry soda

1 cup of strawberry icecream

Strawberry Icecream

Pour into cups.

Blend until smooth.

Enjoy!

# Cup of Worms Rebus

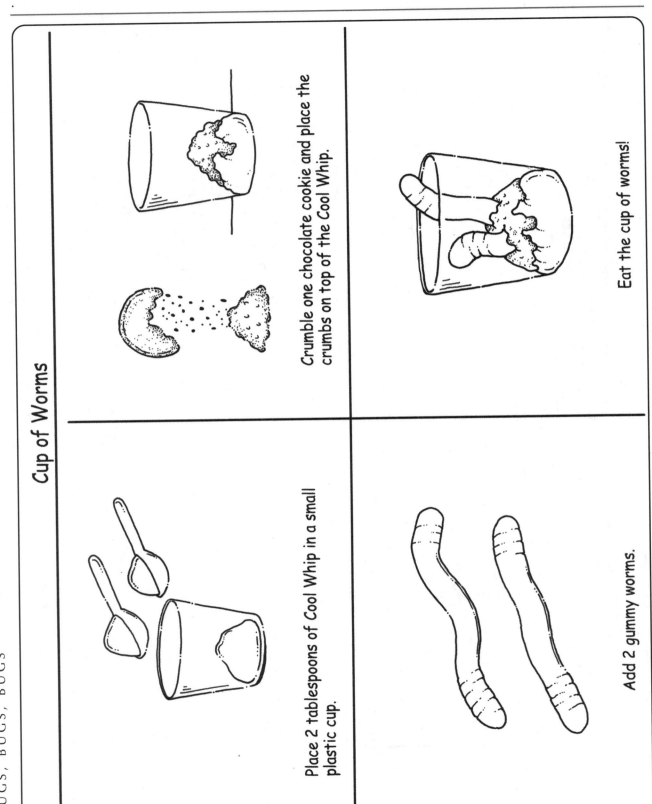

Cup of Worms

Place 2 tablespoons of Cool Whip in a small plastic cup.

Add 2 gummy worms.

Crumble one chocolate cookie and place the crumbs on top of the Cool Whip.

Eat the cup of worms!

# Bessie Bee's Bell Patterns

# Bessie Bee's Bell Patterns

# Bessie Bee's Bell Patterns

# Bessie Bee's Bell Patterns

# Bug Pattern Cards

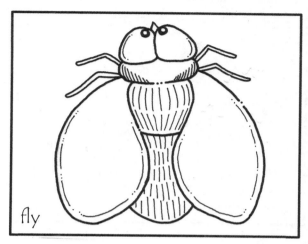

fly

butterfly

ladybug

bee

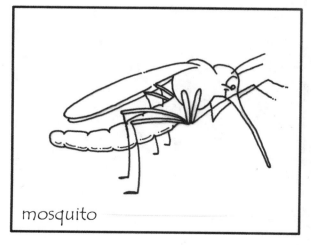

mosquito

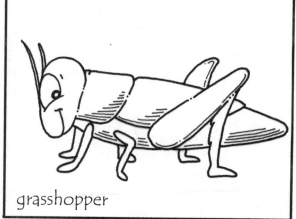

grasshopper

# Bug Pattern Cards

worm

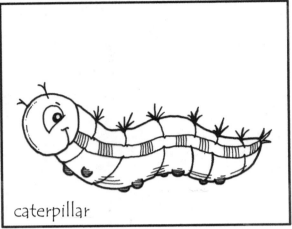

caterpillar

beetle

spider

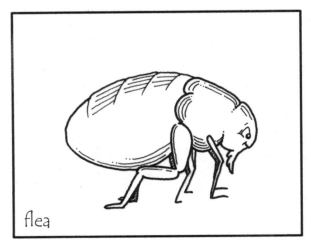

flea

ant

# Over in the Meadow Cards

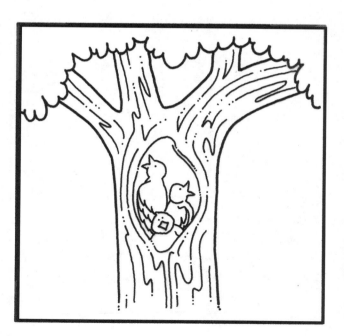

# Over in the Meadow Cards

# Over in the Meadow Cards

# Fly Rhyming Word Game

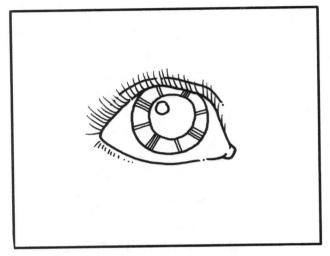

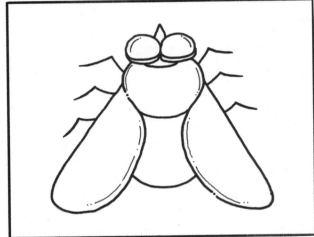

# Ants Go Marching Rhyme Cards

# Mosquito Life Span Sequence Cards

1.

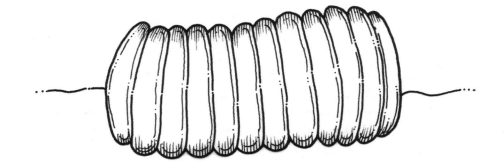

First, the female mosquito drops her eggs into the water.

2.

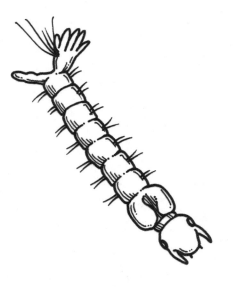

A wriggler hatches from each egg.

# Mosquito Life Span Sequence Cards

3.

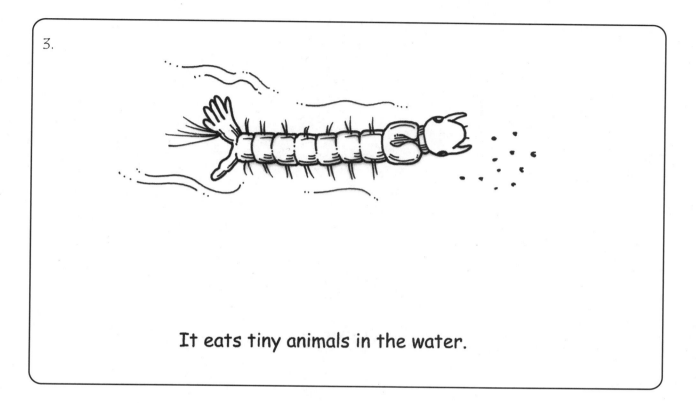

It eats tiny animals in the water.

4.

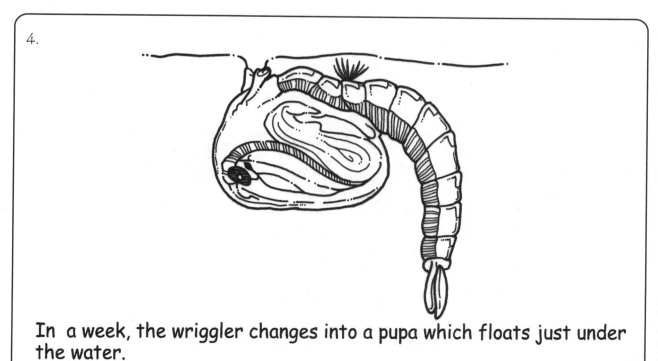

In a week, the wriggler changes into a pupa which floats just under the water.

# Mosquito Life Span Sequence Cards

5.

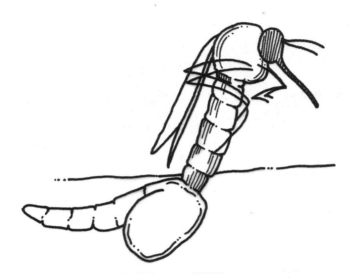

In a few days the pupa's skin splits down the back.

6.

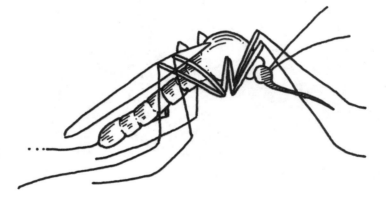

A winged adult mosquito comes out.

# Metamorphosis Sequence Cards

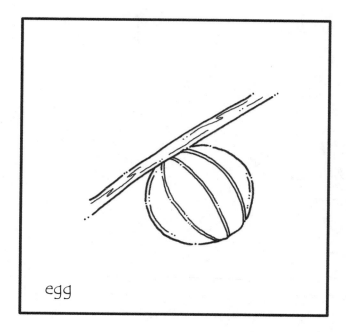

egg

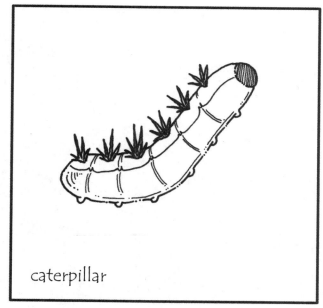

caterpillar

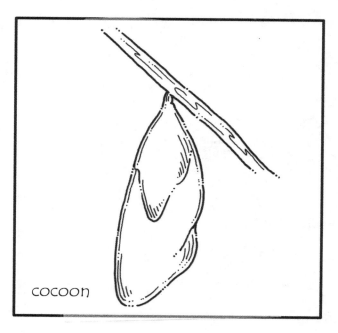

cocoon

butterfly

# Itsy Bitsy Spider Sequence Cards

# Itsy Bitsy Spider Sequence Cards

# Rebus Insect Checklist

☐ 3 body parts

☐ 6 legs

☐ 2 antennae

☐ an outer skeleton

# Venn Diagram

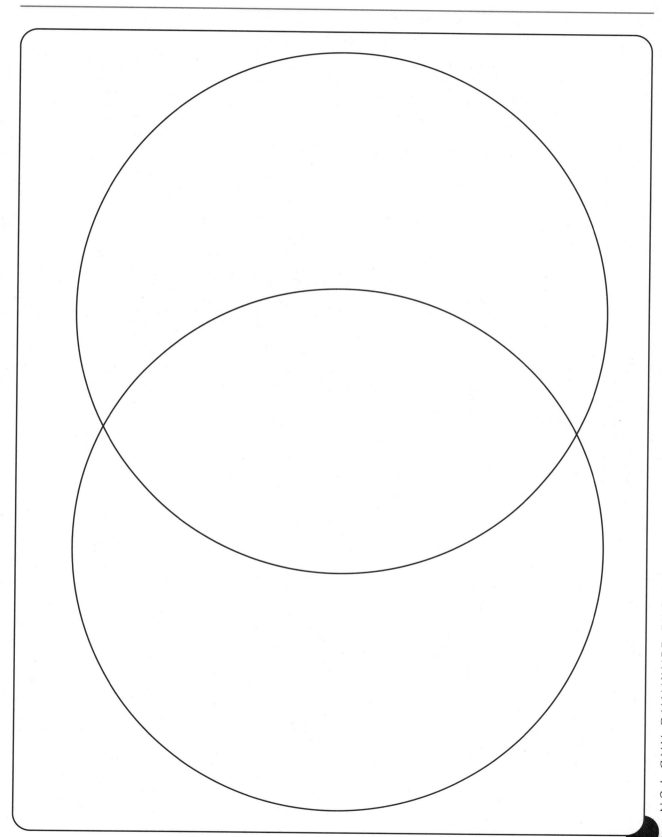

# KWL chart

## KWL Chart

| What We Know | What We Want to Know | What We Learned |
| --- | --- | --- |
|  |  |  |

# American Sign Language Signs

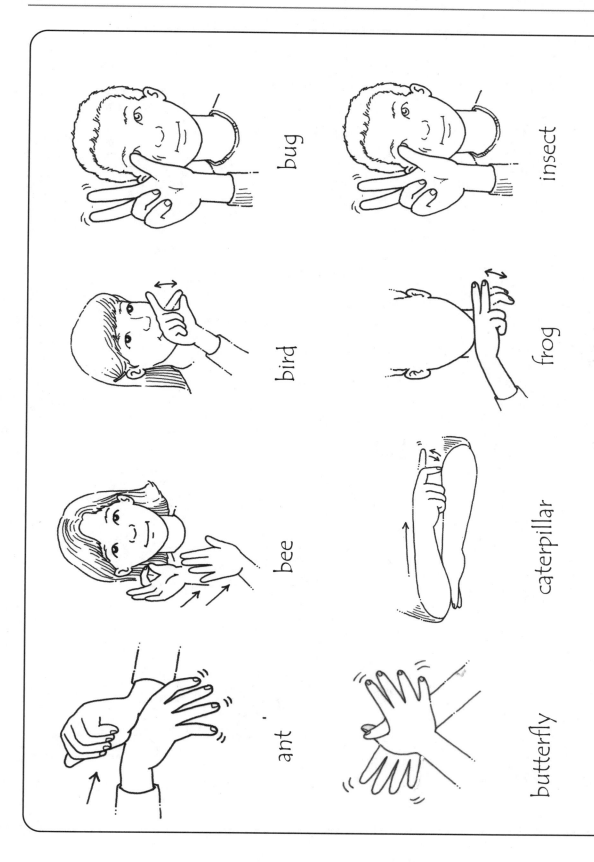

bug

insect

bird

frog

bee

caterpillar

ant

butterfly

# American Sign Language Signs

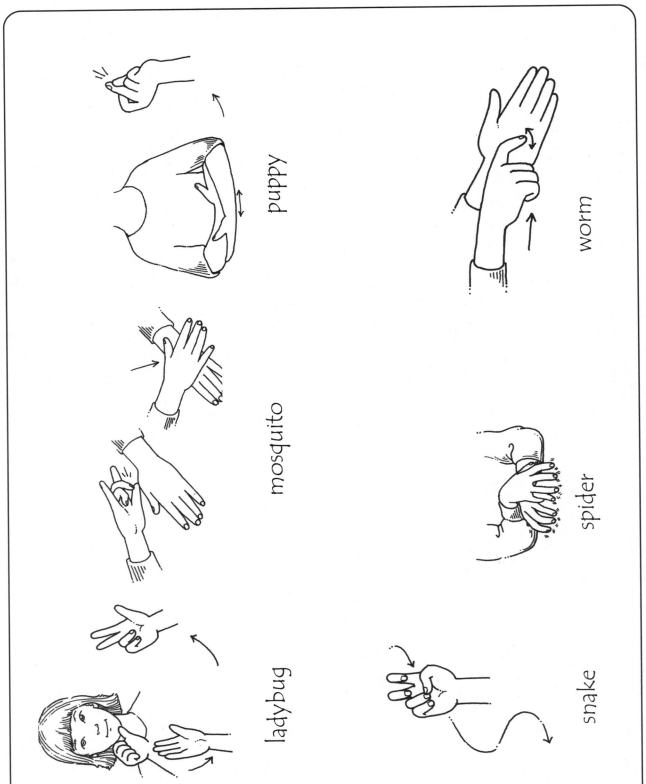

puppy

worm

mosquito

spider

ladybug

snake

# References and Bibliography

Bulloch, K. 2003. *The mystery of modifying: Creative solutions.* Huntsville, TX: Education Service Center, Region VI.

Cavallaro, C. & M. Haney. 1999. *Preschool inclusion.* Baltimore, MD: Paul H. Brookes Publishing Company.

Gray, T. and S. Fleischman. Dec. 2004-Jan. 2005. "Research matters: Successful strategies for English language learners." *Educational Leadership,* 62, 84-85.

Hanniford, C. 1995. *Smart moves: Why learning is not all in your head.* Arlington, VA: Great Ocean Publications, p. 146.

Keller, M. 2004. "Warm weather boosts mood, broadens the mind." *Post Doctoral Study: The University of Michigan,* Anne Arbor, MI.

LeDoux, J. 1993. "Emotional memory systems in the brain." *Behavioral and Brain Research,* 58.

Tabors, P. 1997. *One child, two languages: Children learning English as a second language.* Baltimore, MD: Paul H. Brookes Publishing Co.

# Theme Index

# Children's Book Index

# Index